From Rapture to Revelation

From Rapture to Revelation
Addressing the Spiritual and Theological
Concerns of Former Fundamentalists
in the United States of America

Michelle Grace Lyerly

Wipf & Stock Publishers
Eugene, Oregon

FROM RAPTURE TO REVELATION: ADDRESSING THE SPIRITUAL AND THEOLOGICAL CONCERNS OF FORMER FUNDAMENTALISTS IN THE UNITED STATES OF AMERICA

Copyright © 2006 Michelle Grace Lyerly. All rights reserved. Except for brief quotations in critical publications or reviews, no part of this book may be reproduced in any manner without prior written permission from the publisher. Write: Permissions, Wipf & Stock, 199 W. 8th Ave., Suite 3, Eugene, OR 97401.

ISBN: 1-59752-818-8

Manufactured in the U.S.A.

This research project has been elaborated
under the supervision and coordination of

Prof. Elizabeth S. Tapia,
The Ecumenical Institute of Bossey

and

Prof. Pierre-Yves Brandt,
The Autonomous Faculty of Protestant Theology
of the University of Geneva

Reader: Prof. Gosbert Byamungu,
Ecumenical Institute Bossey

Dedication

To Dr. Paul A. Crow, Jr. and the countless others
who made my studies at the
Ecumenical Institute Bossey possible…

To Dr. Henry Sturcke, a "former fundamentalist"
who showed me that it is possible to find healing
from my past experiences…

To Swami Agnivesh, in whom I have truly encountered
the face of Christ…

…and to Frans Elders, with love.

Table of Contents

Abstract   xi

Chapter One: An Introduction to this Study   1
    Defining Terms   2
    The Reason for this Study   6
    Assumptions of the Author   8
    Protestant Fundamentalism in the United States of America:
       Establishing the Context   9
    Review of Literature   12
    Central Objective and Methodology of this Research   14
    Scope and Limitations of this Research   18

Chapter Two: A Historical Overview of United States Protestant Fundamentalism And a Critical Review of Various American Fundamentalist Movements   20
    John Nelson Darby: The Father of Modern
       Dispensationalism   25
    The Millerites: An Earlier Example of Millennial Obsession   29
    The Prophecies of Ellen G. White:
       The Continuation of Millerite Apocalypticism   32

The Born-Again Movement: A Conservative Reaction Against Theological Liberalism	33
From the Born-Again Theology of Billy Graham to the 1970's Charismatic Movement	35
The Doomsday Prophets of the 1970's: From Books to Films	37
The 1980's: The Decade of the New Religious Right	41
Moving Towards 1999: The Millennial Scare Resurfaces On the American Frontier	42
Concluding Remarks	45

Chapter Three: Evangelicals and Non-Evangelicals in Dialogue: An Overview of the Official Bilateral Dialogues in Relation to the Issues of Biblical Interpretation & Eschatology — 47

Evangelicals and Non-Evangelicals: Reaching a Common Understanding of Biblical Interpretation	48
Methods of Biblical Interpretation and Their Influence on Eschatological Approaches: A Focus on the Seventh-day Adventists and the Lutherans	54
The Baptist/Reformed Contribution	59
The Seventh-Day Adventists and the World Council of Churches: Working Towards a Responsible Eschatology	60

Chapter Four: Conclusion and Implications for Ministry and Ecumenical Relations — 64

A Brief Review of the Project Thus Far	64
The Next Step: Ministering to the Spiritual and Theological Concerns Of Former Fundamentalists in the United States	67
Part I: Dealing With Issues of Biblical Interpretation	67
A Sample Bible Study	70
Part II: Confronting Apocalyptic Enthusiasts from a Distant and More Recent Past	74
Part III: Christological Issues	76
Part IV: Developing a Responsible Eschatology	80

A Ministry of Reconciliation: Going Beyond
    Theological Issues to the Heart of the Matter   82
Final Synopsis and Recommendations for Further Study   87

Bibliography   90

Abbreviations List:
  CGRT - Continuum Glossary of Religious Terms
  EMMM - Encyclopedia of Milliennialism and Millennial Movements
    EF - Encyclopedia of Fundamentalism
   HEC - Harpercollins Enclyclopedia of Catholicism

Abstract

Ever since the September 11, 2001 attacks on the World Trade Center in New York City, there has been a renewed interest in the area of Islamic fundamentalism. Consequently, the interest in Christian fundamentalism has shifted into the background, as it had been a chief concern of a number of authors since the 1970's. In 1993, the World Alliance of Reformed Churches (WARC), the Lutheran World Federation (LWF), and the Pontifical Council for Promoting Christian Unity (PCPCU) conducted a multilateral dialogue addressing the worldwide phenomena of Christian fundamentalism, and they eventually published a report on their findings entitled *Christian Fundamentalism Today: The Papers and Findings of the WARC, LWF, PCPCU Consultation, 22-26 February 1993* (ed. H.S. Wilson, Geneva: World Alliance of Reformed Churches, 1994). While such writings serve to inform the reader on the issue of Christian fundamentalism, they offer no practical steps on how ecumenically minded Christians can more effectively address the spiritual and theological concerns of those who are seeking refuge from the fundamentalist worldview, especially within the context of the United States. This research project will focus on the problem of how ecumenically minded Christians could more effectively address the spiritual and theological concerns of former fundamentalists in the United States, especially when dealing with the difficult theological topics of biblical inerrancy and eschatology. Since evangelicals closely resemble fundamentalists in doctrine and practice, the author will approach this task by conducting a textual analysis of the documents that came out of some of the official bilateral dialogues between evangelicals and non-evangelical groups in hopes that the results of these documents will offer some clues as to how to improve relations between former fundamentalists and ecumenically minded Christians, especially when it comes to dealing with the aforementioned theological issues.

Chapter One
An Introduction to this Study

Ever since the September 11, 2001 attacks on the World Trade Center in New York City, there has been a renewed interest in the area of Islamic fundamentalism. Consequently, the interest in Christian fundamentalism has shifted into the background, as it had been a chief concern of a number of authors since the 1970's. In 1993, the World Alliance of Reformed Churches (WARC), the Lutheran World Federation (LWF), and the Pontifical Council for Promoting Christian Unity (PCPCU) conducted a multilateral dialogue addressing the worldwide phenomena of Christian fundamentalism, and they eventually published a report on their findings entitled *Christian Fundamentalism Today*.[1] While this report, along with a number of other writings, serve to inform the reader on the issue of Christian fundamentalism, they offer no practical steps on how ecumenically minded Christians can more effectively address the spiritual and theological concerns of those who are seeking refuge from the fundamentalist worldview, especially within the context of the United States.

Since Christian fundamentalists are often wary of the World Council of Churches, and the Ecumenical Movement, in general, there has been

---

[1] *Christian Fundamentalism Today: The Papers and Findings of the WARC, LWF, PCPCU Consultation, 22 to 26 February 1993*, ed. H.S. Wilson (Geneva: World Alliance of Reformed Churches, 1994).

very little contact between the two camps. It has been the experience and observation of this author that most moderate and liberal Christians are not sure how to react towards the exclusivist nature of such religious groups, and this is mainly due to their lack of understanding of the theological worldview of U.S. Protestant fundamentalism. While the author feels that many ecumenically minded Christians truly desire to help former fundamentalists come to terms with their past, they most likely find such a task difficult, because they struggle to understand the possible bearing that the fundamentalist worldview can have on the life of the adherent in terms of how one relates to God and the world. Consequently, they also do not understand the emotional scars that emerging from such a worldview can leave on the life of the individual. Therefore, whenever ecumenically minded Christians come into contact with former fundamentalists who report their struggles with the exclusivist nature of the fundamentalist worldview, the former group does not know how to effectively address the concerns of those who have emerged from the influence of fundamentalism.

This research project will focus on the problem of how ecumenically minded Christians could more effectively address the spiritual and theological concerns of former fundamentalists in the United States, especially when dealing with the difficult theological topics of biblical inerrancy and eschatology. Since evangelicals closely resemble fundamentalists in doctrine and practice, the author will approach this task by doing a textual analysis of the documents that came out of some of the official bilateral dialogues between evangelicals and non-evangelical groups in hopes that the results of these documents will offer some clues as to how to improve relations between former fundamentalists and ecumenically minded Christians, especially when it comes to dealing with the aforementioned theological concerns.

Defining Terms

Fundamentalism is an ongoing struggle to maintain the ideals of the past in the face of the challenges of progress. In other words, it is symptomatic of a denial on behalf of an individual or a group of people to accept the personal and cultural growth that progress brings as communities grow and change, and it is accompanied by a refusal to adapt ideological and religious symbols in accordance with such changes. Fundamentalists are quick to "...select what in modernity is evil to characterize the *entire* 'modern times' and then they compare it with a reconstructed idealized earlier *Golden Age*, by selecting and emphasizing one or other of its traits, which they regard as doctrinal and practical fundamentals for the present."[2] Fundamentalism does not need to be religious; it can also be ideological or political. However, all ideologies take on a religious character, even if they deny the existence of an ultimate being, because ideologies themselves claim some level of objective validity.

According to Phil Hughes, a Canadian who maintains a website devoted to the potential dangers of religious fundamentalism: "Fundamentalism is to the spirit as cancer is to the body, a diseased parody of growth that makes death a welcome release. If we are looking for 'dark powers,' this is where we will find them most readily, not in 'dens of iniquity,' but within the precincts of temple, church, and mosque."[3] Similarly, as early as 1983, James Barr, a Hebrew professor at Oxford University, wrote:

> Since I first began to write about it, additional experience through a multitude of letters and personal contacts has much reinforced the deep sense of pain and personal suffering that fundamentalism often occasions. The alienation between people that it brings about is extreme. Lay people come to regard their minister as 'unsound' or worse…For thousands of people the question of fundamentalism is their central personal religious problem. And, on the world-wide scale, when one looks at the social and political implications, few can doubt what many observers have noted: that the continuance of religious fundamentalism, and of the attitudes associated with it, may have great importance in determining whether or not mankind [*sic*] is to be destroyed through nuclear warfare.[4]

---

[2] Thomas F. Stransky, "Fundamentalists, Protestant & Catholic: An Ecumenical Challenge?" in *Christian Fundamentalism Today: The Papers and Findings of the WARC, LWF, PCPCU Consultation, 22 to 26 February 1993*, ed. H.S. Wilson (Geneva: World Alliance of Reformed Churches, 1994), 22-39: 26.
[3] Phil Hughes, "Paths: The Way of the Soul," in "The Telson Spur: Field Nodes-Paths 7," via *Internet* (British Columbia: Canada, 21 Feb. 2005), <http://www.snark.org/~pjhughes/ate3.htm>. Accessed March 4, 2005.
[4] James Barr, *Escaping from Fundamentalism* (London: SCM Press Ltd., 1984), ix-x.

One does not have to look very far to see the damage that is caused by religious fundamentalism (of all faith traditions): the fall of the Twin Towers, the war in Iraq, and the emergence of various religious cults and sects in the United States, such the Branch Davidians of Texas, the Heaven's Gate cult, and various millennial cults and sects that emerged as a result of the recent "Y2K scare."[5] Whenever any person or group takes a literalistic approach to any ideology or teaching, whether that teaching be religious or not, trouble will most likely ensue, because a strict religious interpretation presents stringent limitations on the committed follower.

Christian fundamentalism is a multifaceted phenomenon. Christian fundamentalist sects can be identified from among all Christian confessional traditions: Roman Catholic, Orthodox, and the various Protestant denominations. Due to time and space limitations, the central focus of this research project will be Protestant fundamentalism in the United States of America. The *Continuum Glossary of Religious Terms* defines American Christian fundamentalism as:

> American EVANGELICAL movements created out of opposition to secularization in the second half of the twentieth century. Fundamentalism is characterized by its literalness in scriptural interpretation and animosity to any form of biblical criticism. It asserts the immanent return of Christ before the end of time.[6]

However, it must be noted that not all evangelicals are fundamentalists. While fundamentalists and evangelicals make similar claims regarding issues such as the authority of scripture and the urgent need to evangelize the world,[7] the fundamentalist group "…operates by identifying its

---

[5] The "Y2K scare" pertains to a fear that due to the limited number of digits in the clocks of computers, all the computers in the world that were not "Y2K compliant" would crash. Many fundamentalists were afraid that this event would lead to a worldwide catastrophe, which would set the stage for worldwide reception of a mighty political leader who would become the Antichrist.

[6] Author(s) Unknown, "Fundamentalism: *Christianity*" in *Continuum Glossary of Religious Terms*, ed. Ron Geaves (London: New York: Continuum, 2002), 119.

[7] *The Harpercollins Encyclopedia of Catholicism* defines evangelicalism as "…an interdenominational Protestant movement dedicated to spreading the gospel to non-Christians and revitalizing faith among non-Christians. Evangelicalism emphasizes

sponsors with the absolute, raises an exclusive claim to truth, validity and domination, and aims at subjecting or even eliminating whatever is different from itself."[8] On the whole, evangelicals tend to be more tolerant of other Christian belief systems[9] and are more willing to engage in ecumenical dialogue. Fundamentalist groups, on the other hand, have the tendency to be intolerant of other faiths and ideologies, and they maintain narrow moral and doctrinal codes to which their followers are expected to adhere.

For the purposes of this research, "ecumenically minded Christians" are those Christians who are willing to engage in ecumenical dialogue, even if they do not understand other denominations to be full members of the larger Christian community. The term "ecumenically minded Christians" does not only refer to Christians beyond the evangelical tradition, but it includes evangelicals who are more receptive of other expressions of the Christian faith. The fact that any Christian group is willing to consider the views of the "other" shows some level of commitment to the greater unity of all Christendom. This receptive attitude distinguishes all ecumenically minded Christians from fundamentalists, who are defined by their refusal to consider validity of the viewpoints of all other Christian groups.

The references, which are made to either "spiritual concerns" or "theological concerns," encompass the religious struggles and questions that present themselves whenever one makes a decision to reject the fundamentalist worldview. Anyone who comes out of a fundamentalist tradition will most likely testify to its narrow treatment of certain theological topics, such as the nature of God and the relationship of God to the world, and consequently, one will face struggles in the attempt to emerge from that worldview. The issues of biblical interpretation and

---

individual conversion (the 'new birth') to a personal, experienced faith in Christ; Christ's atoning sacrifice for individual sin; the Bible's authority in matters of faith and life; holy living; and the obligation of laity and clergy to propagate the gospel through preaching and missionary effort." [Michael S. Hamilton, "Evangelicalism" in *HEC*, eds. Richard P. McBrien, et al (San Francisco: HarperCollins Publishers, 1995), 492-493]. For a more complete definition of "evangelical," see also "Evangelical: *Christianity*," in *CGRT*, 113 (Author(s) Unknown).

[8] Heinrich Schafer, "A Conservative Evangelical Perspective" in *Christian Fundamentalism Today*, 64-83: 83.

[9] Hamilton, "Evangelicalism," in *HEC*, 493.

eschatology, or "last things," cannot be separated from the aforementioned religious and theological concerns, but are integral to the way that a religious group expresses its belief in God and its approach to world events. Therefore, these two issues will be the chief theological concerns that will be addressed within this research.

The first issue, the approach to biblical interpretation, deals primarily with the nature of God, as it examines how closely God is tied to the holy scriptures of that tradition. It asks whether or not God is viewed as the definitive author of the scriptures, and if the answer to this question is affirmative, there is to be no level of compromise in dealing with methods of biblical interpretation (the doctrine of inerrancy). If God is viewed by the group as having allowed any margin-of-error in the processes of transcription and translation of the texts-in-question, then there is usually more freedom allowed in the act of scriptural interpretation. The way that a religious group deals with these issues has an undeniable impact upon its view of the relationship of God to the world: if God rules the world with a proverbial "iron fist," or if God relates to the world in a more realistic and forgiving fashion.

The answers that are provided to the above questions will undoubtedly influence the way that the religious group-in-question approaches eschatological issues, which deal with the matters of final judgment and eventual establishment of the Reign of God on earth. For a religious group which views the world as the arena of divine rewards and punishments, such an uncompromising perspective will most likely have a negative impact on how that religious group approaches God and relates to the larger world. Such are the spiritual concerns that will be addressed within this research, as the author searches for ways to promote healing and reconciliation among people who are struggling to emerge from the fundamentalist worldview and are seeking the aide of their ecumenically minded sisters and brothers in the process of doing so.

The Reason For this Study

The author of this study describes herself as a recovering fundamentalist from the conservative Southeastern United States. Although she was very active in her local Southern Baptist congregation and attended two fundamentalist schools from the preschool years until eighth grade, she became frustrated in her attempt to establish a connection with God. The emphasis within the church on having a proper personal "salvation experience" and endless talk about the "Second Coming of Christ" led the author to experience more fear and frustration. The claims from the pulpit regarding biblical inerrancy only led the author to conclude that the decision to reject this worldview would lead to inevitable damnation.

During her junior high school years, the author attended a small fundamentalist school that only reinforced her deep-seated fears. During one of the Bible classes at this school, one of the teachers showed a film series based on Darbyite Dispensationalism to this impressionable group of twelve-year-olds about life during the "Great Tribulation." These films contained graphic scenes that are not too far removed from some of the footage seen in documentaries of Nazi Germany. The images presented in this film left the author traumatized for many years and led to frequent nightmares, anxiety attacks, and even some level of paranoia.

Around the turn of the millennium, the author encountered a fringe group of Pentecostals who taught that the "Y2K scare" would bring about a state of global chaos or the "Great Tribulation" that would inaugurate the millennial reign of Christ. Given the strong influence of this film and the strong emphasis that her denomination placed upon the reality of these eschatological events, the author fell prey to the exclusivist claims of this millennialist group. The encounter with this group led to further psychological complications, which could only have been cured through therapy, theological studies in a liberal institution, and encounters with other Christians who were more tolerant of highly complex theological and philosophical inquiry.

Since this incident, the author has met other American Christians who have reported similar experiences and have sought refuge from the fundamentalist worldview. Therefore, the author feels that there is a need to invite ecumenically minded Christians to become more aware of this issue, so that they can more effectively minister to the theological concerns of former fundamentalists who seek spiritual refuge in more theologically progressive churches. Former fundamentalists need to be reassured that there is not just one valid expression of the Christian faith, and that the presence of God can also be found in other denominations that do not share in the fundamentalist worldview.

Assumptions of the Author

This project operates under many assumptions, of which the author will attempt to substantiate throughout this research. One assumption is that fundamentalism is a binding force in the life of individual adherents. Since the author was raised in a strict fundamentalist atmosphere in the Southeastern United States, which is commonly referred to as the "Bible Belt," the reflections of this research pertaining to fundamentalism already contain a certain level of negative bias. The reality is that fundamentalism may not be as authoritarian as the author assumes. Therefore, those who leave fundamentalist denominations might not need assistance from their ecumenical sisters and brothers in finding a more holistic worldview. They most likely just need to find a religious community that more clearly expresses the conclusions that they have already reached through personal analysis and research.

Fundamentalism can provide positive experiences for people who need a certain level of theological certainty and connection with the transcendent, support from like-minded individuals, and a strong sense of purpose and direction in life. Not every experience with fundamentalism is potentially harmful, and the ecumenical Christian must be aware of the positive elements that exist within fundamentalist Christianity that will help enhance the future of Christendom and provide an positive sense of security to those who are seeking refuge from fundamentalist influence, but are not quite ready to leave all of the comforts of their former religious lives.

The second assumption of the author is that ecumenically minded Christians do not understand the struggles of former fundamentalists and often dismiss their struggles as insignificant. The reality is that many denominations that are more ecumenically oriented are often composed of former fundamentalists who have struggled with similar issues and have sought freedom from their former denominations. The Cooperative Baptist Fellowship within the United States is one example of a denomination that has emerged as a result of the fundamentalist takeover of the Southern Baptist Convention. This denomination is evangelical in nature, but it takes a more liberal stance on biblical authority and social issues. The Christian Church (Disciples of Christ), a denomination that is not evangelical in nature and also tends to be more liberal in its stances on biblical authority and social issues. However, it serves as a refuge for many former fundamentalists who are seeking a more holistic theology that embraces a modernistic worldview. Many former evangelicals and fundamentalists alike are drawn to this denomination due to its practice of adult baptism, which can be found in most evangelical and fundamentalist denominations.

Protestant Fundamentalism in the United States of America: Establishing the Context

Often referred to as the "great experiment,"[10] the United States is a country that was founded upon religious freedom, due to a need to break away from perceived corruption within the various established European religious systems. Religious refugees saw the move to this uncharted land as a golden opportunity to seize the land in the name of God. In their efforts to establish a religiously pure nation, immigrants joined forces in seeking to assist in inaugurating the eventual Reign of God on earth. Therefore, the North American religious experience began as a conscious split from traditional forms of religious expression.

As many different religious groups, such as the settlers of Jamestown (1607) and Plymouth Rock (1620)[11] arrived in the "New World," over time, such groups developed their own forms of religious authoritarianism. Although the ideal condition of the "New World" called for the avoidance of establishing a state church, "Most of the early colonies had their own state churches, with New England being predominantly Congregational and the colonies from New York to Georgia ascribing to the Anglican faith."[12] However, once the United States was established, it refrained from declaring a national church. It was not until the drafting of the

---

[10] J. Gordon Melton and Robert L. Moore, *The Cult Experience: Responding to the New Religious Pluralism* (New York: The Pilgrim Press, 1986), 22.

[11] James E. Wood, Jr. "Introduction" in *Baptists and the North American Experience*, ed. James E. Wood, Jr. (Valley Forge, Pennsylvania: Judson Press, 1976), 11.

[12] Melton and Moore, *The Cult Experience*, 22.

Fourteenth Amendment in 1868, that the U.S. Constitution forbade the establishment of any official state church:[13] "No state shall make or enforce any law which shall abridge the privileges or immunities of citizens of the United States; nor shall any state deprive any person of life, liberty, or property, without due process of law; nor deny to any person within its jurisdiction the equal protection of laws."[14]

Such a constitutional provision directly corresponds with the First Amendment of the U.S. Constitution's *Bill of Rights*, which states, "Congress shall make no law respecting an establishment of religion, or prohibiting the free exercise thereof...."[15] However, when the First Amendment was drafted, concerns were centered around the establishment of national law; concerns regarding the individual states developed later as necessity called. Therefore, one can see how individual states could oppress their citizens regarding the establishment of an official state religion without violating the laws regarding the subjection of individuals to an overarching national religion. In reference to the *U.S. Constitution*, Melton and Moore state, "The Constitution protected the 36 churches serving approximately 5 million Americans. It did not, however, prevent individual states from following a particular church."[16]

As these individual state religions required the loyalty of their citizens, many desperate religious renegades traveled west in search of newfound religious freedom. Many of the new religious movements that accompanied western expansion were tailored to meet the emotional and spiritual needs of these new adventure-seekers. Therefore, these new religious movements

---

[13] *Ibid*. According to Melton and Moore, "Thus, in the 1850's the state church of Utah was Mormon" (p. 22). This shows how long it took from the initial arrival of the settlers in the 1600's, to the drafting of the Fourteenth Amendment of the U.S. Constitution in 1868. (See <http://www.law.cornell.edu/constitution.table.html#amendements> for the provision of this date. See below in footnote 14 for a more complete reference to the Legal Information Institute of Cornell University.), to abolish the establishment of state churches. [Website accessed March 5, 2005]).

[14] *United States Constitution*, Section 1: Amendment XIV, via *Internet* (LII: Legal Information Institute: Cornell University, Ithaca: New York, n.d.), <http://www.law.cornell.edu/constitution/constitution.amendmentxiv.html>. Accessed March 5, 2005.

[15] *United States Constitution*, Section I: Amendment I, via *Internet* (LII: Legal Information Institute: Cornell University). <http://www.law.cornell.edu/constitution.billofrights.html#amendmeni>. Accessed March 5, 2005.

[16] Melton and Moore, *The Cult Experience*, 22.

An Introduction to this Study

of what is commonly called the "Second Great Awakening" took the form of frenzied revival meetings with a great emphasis placed upon personal conversion experiences.

Over a long period of time, such religious experiences eventually crystallized into separate Christian denominations, each with their own set of doctrines and practices.[17] Due to the evangelistic fervor of their members and the commitment of parents to pass these belief systems on to their children, these type of congregations progressively scattered throughout various portions of the larger United States:

> They set about this task with a vengeance, developing an amazing variety of 'new measures' to assist people in beginning the religious life. These new measures, which spoke directly to the heart and the religious affections (to use Jonathan Edwards' term), became ingrained in the American frontier faith. The measures-revivals, camp meetings, insistence on immediate conversion, the mourner's bench, excited preaching-were passed from one generation to the next by precept and example. Each generation received them, altered them to their particular time and place, perfected them, and took John Wesley's, Jonathan Edwards', and Charles Finney's early statements about them and codified them. By the end of the nineteenth century, evangelists had honed conversion to a fine art.[18]

Given the isolated nature of these frontier denominations from their parent congregations, and the lack of contact with other churches in general, one can easily understand how the members of these congregations would have begun to have believed that their churches had the correct interpretations of the Christian message. Consequently, such denominations have a tendency to become binding to individual adherents who sincerely believe that their particular traditions have monopolies on the truth. Given the exclusive nature of fundamentalist doctrine, many of its adherents are

---

[17] Melton and Moore, *The Cult Experience* 23-24. The authors write, "Called the Second Great Awakening, the revival launched the Baptists, the Methodists, and the Cumberland Presbyterians" (23).

[18] Ibid.,, 23-24. The authors refer the reader to a variety of authors in footnote 10 on page 24.

led to believe that they have no other options, and that if they leave their congregations or question the authority of God's word, as it is interpreted by their denominations, they will be in danger of eternal damnation. Often, the searching, sincere members of these religious groups become frustrated in their attempts to follow the strict teachings of these churches, but they do not know how to address their questions and concerns. For the naturally inquisitive and observant fundamentalist, such straightforward answers do not correspond to the needs of life in modern society.

Whenever these seekers begin to address their questions, other members of their congregations, either consciously or unconsciously, instill fear into the minds of these concerned members for having doubts about their commitment to the "true" Christian faith. For the ones who take the necessary steps to leave these particular congregations, countless emotional consequences can follow, such as feelings of alienation, betrayal and confusion, the inability to reintegrate into modern society, and intense fears of eternal condemnation. For those who are in the process of considering leaving such churches, certain questions often come to mind, such as, "Will I, in leaving fundamentalism, lose the support of biblical authority? And will I, in leaving it, find that I have also lost the core of evangelical religion?"[19]

Review of Literature

The central focus of this research will be United States Protestant fundamentalism. Many authors address fundamentalism in conjunction with evangelicalism, as the line between the two movements can often become extremely blurred, especially within the North American context. The following list of books will prove helpful to anyone who desires to understand the context of United States Protestant fundamentalism and the pervading social and religious factors that wield their influence upon this exclusivist worldview.

In *Born Againism: Perspectives on a Movement*,[20] Eric W. Gritsch, writes about the issue of being "born again," as this experience is found in both

---

[19] Barr, *Escaping from Fundamentalism*, ix.
[20] Eric W. Gritsch, *Born Againism: Perspectives on a Movement* (Philadelphia: Fortress Press, 1982).

An Introduction to this Study

fundamentalist and evangelical circles in the United States. Similarly, James E. Wood, Jr. serves as the editor of a book on North American evangelicalism entitled *Baptists and the North American Experience*.[21] This book explores the contributions that Baptists have made to the overall shaping of American religious and political landscape. Other authors, such as George M. Mardsen in *Fundamentalism and American Culture*[22] and Ernest R. Sandeen in *The Roots of Fundamentalism: British and American Millenarianism 1800-1930*,[23] focus more exclusively on the phenomenon of Protestant fundamentalism as it combats the perceived threats of modernity.

The above list is not exhaustive; however it includes a central core of literature that covers the issue of United States Protestant fundamentalism. For further information on North American Protestant fundamentalism from a native of the Southeastern United States (commonly referred to as the "Bible Belt), one should consult *Rescuing the Bible from Fundamentalism: A Bishop Rethinks the Meaning of Scripture*[24] by John Shelby Spong, an Anglican Bishop who currently resides and works in Newark, New Jersey. In his book, he addresses how it is still possible for one to take the biblical texts seriously without resorting to the destructive doctrine of biblical inerrancy. Another relevant work includes *The Book of Jerry Falwell: Fundamentalist Language and Politics*[25] by Susan F. Harding, which deals with the mindset of the "Religious Right" in America, and she spends a great deal of time on the issue of conversion, or in fundamentalist terms, being "born again." Another work that is written in the same line of thought is *Onward Christian Soldiers? The Religious Right in American*

---

[21] James E. Wood, Jr., ed. *Baptists and the American Experience* (Valley Forge, Pennsylvania: Judson Press, 1976). It should be noted that some Baptist groups can properly be classified as fundamentalist, but many Baptist groups are simply evangelicals.

[22] George M. Marsden, *Fundamentalism and American Culture: The Shaping of Twentieth Century Evangelicalism, 1870-1925* (New York/Oxford: Oxford University Press, 1980).

[23] Ernest R. Sandeen, *The Roots of Fundamentalism: British and American Millenarianism, 1800-1930* (Grand Rapids: Baker Book House, 1978).

[24] John Shelby Spong, *Rescuing the Bible from Fundamentalism: A Bishop Rethinks the Meaning of Scripture* (New York: HarperCollins Publishers, 1991).

[25] Susan Friend Harding, *The Book of Jerry Falwell: Fundamentalist Language and Politics* (Princeton: Princeton University Press, 2000).

Politics[26] by Clyde Wilcox. This work addresses the influence of the religious right on the American political scene during the 1980's and early 1990's. Moreover, while all of these works prove helpful in the attempt to understand the historical dimensions of United States fundamentalism and the potential consequences of the fundamentalist worldview, the author has not found any literature that deals with how to bridge the gaps between the two groups-in-question, and more specifically, turning to past bilateral ecumenical dialogues between evangelicals and non-evangelicals in order to search for answers on how to accomplish the aforementioned goal.

On the contrary, Don Feder's book, *Who's Afraid of the Religious Right?*,[27] presents a well-reasoned counterargument to the position of the majority of authors regarding the Religious Right. As a self-avowed religious Jew, he presents what he sees as the positive aspects and contributions of the Religious Right to American society. Another book that proves helpful in this discussion is *How My Mind Has Changed: Thirteen Distinguished Religious Thinkers Assess the Impact of the Last Decade on their Lives and Thought*,[28] which is edited by Harold E. Fey. This book includes an essay by the American evangelist Rev. Billy Graham, whose simplistic approach to Christianity will be examined within chapter two. In this essay, which was written at a later point in his ministry, Rev. Graham talks about how his encounters with other Christians throughout various parts of the world have changed his thoughts on the nature of God and the issue of soteriology, or salvation.[29]

Central Objective and Methodology of this Research

After one leaves a fundamentalist sect, one often feels alone and scared. The perplexed fundamentalist will often leave the denomination with

---

[26] Clyde Wilcox, *Onward Christian Soldiers?: The Religious Right in American Politics*. Dilemmas in American Politics: Series Editor: L. Sandy Maisel (Boulder, Colorado/Oxford, United Kingdom: Westview Press, 1996).

[27] Don Feder, *Who's Afraid of the Religious Right?* (Washington, D.C.: Regnery Publishing, Inc., 1996).

[28] Harold E. Fey, *How My Mind Has Changed: Thirteen Distinguished Religious Thinkers Assess the Impact of the Last Decade on Their Lives and Thought*, Living Age Books, Consulting Editor Marvin P. Halverson (Cleveland, Ohio and New York: Meridian Books, The World Publishing Company, 1961).

[29] Billy Graham, "Billy Graham" in *How My Mind Has Changed*, 55-68.

many unanswered questions. Sometimes, one will leave Christianity, or even religion, altogether. Many who do not want to leave the church atmosphere will join what is referred to as "post-church groups,"[30] which operate like group therapy sessions, in that they provide an open forum for former evangelicals and fundamentalists to discuss topics that they felt were forbidden to discuss in their previous churches. Others will seek refuge in non-fundamentalist Christian denominations, which claim to be more accepting and ecumenically minded. It has been the experience and observation of the author of this research project that many ecumenically minded Christians do not seem to know how to effectively address the concerns of former fundamentalists, especially when it comes to the theological issues of biblical inerrancy and eschatology. They do not seem to understand why these people struggle with feelings of alienation, fear, betrayal, or sometimes suffer from even worse psychological complications.

Therefore, this research project will address the issue of how ecumenically minded Christians can more effectively address the spiritual and theological concerns of former fundamentalists. Since evangelicals most closely resemble fundamentalists in doctrine and practice, with the exception of being more ecumenically minded, this project will conduct a textual analysis of a number of reports that emerged out of official bilateral dialogues held between evangelical and non-evangelical Christian denominations. It is the belief of this author that a thorough examination of how these official bilateral dialogues deal with the issues of biblical interpretation and eschatology can offer important insights as to how ecumenically minded Christians could more effectively address the spiritual and theological concerns of former fundamentalists in the United States. This research seeks to provide answers to the central question of how ecumenically minded Christians can develop more sensitivity to the past religious experiences of former fundamentalists, and in effect, help promote healing and reconciliation in their lives. The likelihood is that many ecumenical Christians have difficulty responding to the spiritual

---

[30] Alan Jamieson, "Churchless Faith: Trajectories of Faith Beyond the Church From Evangelical, Pentecostal, and Charismatic Churches to Post-Church Groups" in *International Review of Mission*, ed. Jacqus Matthey, v.. 92, no. 365 (Geneva: WCC Publications, 2003), 217-226: 222. Jamieson is a Baptist minister in New Zealand.

and theological concerns of former fundamentalists, because they do not have a thorough understanding of the struggles that these people have undergone throughout the course of their religious development.

The second chapter will provide a more in-depth historical overview of the development of North American Protestant fundamentalist and evangelical doctrine and practice in the United States. This section will introduce the reader to the beginnings and basic doctrinal elements of United States fundamentalist denominations and the pervading social and intellectual issues of that time that fueled their development. The second chapter will serve as a link to the third chapter, as it will provide the reader with a general basis for understanding the basic belief systems and historical contexts of the evangelical[31] denominations that will be presented within chapter three. Throughout the second chapter, the author will also attempt to address the potential negative impact of the fundamentalist worldview on the life of the sincere believer. Much emphasis within this chapter will be placed on the doctrine of biblical inerrancy and United States millennial obsession. In focusing on these two key elements of American Protestant fundamentalist belief, this chapter will seek to demonstrate how these two beliefs can promote fear and anxiety in the life of the sincere fundamentalist devotee.

The third chapter will provide a textual analysis of the documents related to official consultations between certain evangelical and non-evangelical denominations in order to provide a basis for the final conclusions of the research regarding how ecumenically minded Christians could more effectively address the spiritual and theological concerns of former Protestant fundamentalist Christians in the United States, especially in regards to the issues of biblical interpretation and eschatology. One of the practical steps that are included in such a textual analysis will be a careful reading of the texts in order to see how the official reports deal with the issues of biblical interpretation and eschatology. After exploring and reporting on how the reports handle these issues, any connections that can be drawn from among the reports regarding the aforementioned theological issues will be

---

[31] Once again, it should be noted that evangelical groups resemble fundamentalist groups in belief and practice, and many fundamentalists are evangelical. The main distinction between the two groups is that non-fundamentalist evangelical groups are more open to other expressions of Christianity. Often the line between fundamentalism and evangelicalism becomes extremely blurry. This reality will undoubtedly present some difficulties in this research.

An Introduction to this Study

indicated within this research. This textual analysis will provide a basis for any conclusions that are reached throughout this study.

The primary sources that will be consulted within the third chapter include the official reports from a series of bilateral dialogues conducted between the Baptist World Alliance (BWA) and the World Alliance of Reformed Churches (WARC), entitled *Baptists and Reformed in Dialogue: Documents from the Conversations Sponsored by the World Alliance of Reformed Churches and the Baptist World Alliance*[32] and the report from the Lutheran/Adventist consultations that were held between 1994-1998, which are entitled *Lutherans & Adventists in Conversation: Report and Papers Presented 1994-1998*.[33] Other sources to which occasional reference will be made as needed include, but are not limited to, various documents related to consultations in the early seventies between the World Council of Churches and the Seventh-day Adventists,[34] the WCC and the Pentecostals in the Americas,[35] and a document pertaining to the participation of the Assemblies of God within the Ecumenical Movement.[36]

---

[32] Editor(s) Unknown, World Alliance of Reformed Churches, *Baptists and Reformed in Dialogue: Documents from the Conversations Sponsored by the World Alliance of Reformed Churches and the Baptist World Alliance* (Geneva: World Alliance of Reformed Churches, 1984).

[33] Editor(s) Unknown, General Conference of Seventh-day Adventists and the Lutheran World Federation, *Lutherans & Adventists in Conversation: Report and Papers Presented 1994-1998* (General Conference of Seventh-day Adventists: Silver Springs Maryland, USA and Geneva, Switzerland: The Lutheran World Federation, 2000).

[34] Editor(s) Unknown, Faith and Order Commission, World Council of Churches, *The World Council of Churches/Seventh-Day Adventist Conversations and their Significance*, Faith and Order Papers No. 55/Reprinted from *The Ecumenical Review* Vol. XXII No. 2-April 1970 (Switzerland, n.d.), Editor(s) Unknown, Faith and Order Commission, World Council of Churches, The World Council of Churches/Seventh-Day Adventist Conversations: Meetings in 1970 and 1971, Faith and Order Paper No. 62/Reprinted from *The Ecumenical Review* Vol. XXIV No. 2-April 1972 (Switzerland, n.d.), and Editor(s) Unknown, World Council of Churches, *So Much in Common: Documents of Interest in the Conversations Between the World Council of Churches and the Seventh-day Adventist Church* (Geneva: World Council of Churches, 1973).

[35] Editor(s) Unknown, Office of Church and Ecumenical Relations, World Council of Churches, *Consultation with Pentecostal Churches: Lima, Peru 14 to 19 November 1994* (Bialystok: Poland: Orthdruk Orthodox Printing House, n.d.) and Huibert van Beek, ed., *Consultation with Pentecostals in the Americas: San Jose, Costa Rica 4-8 June 1996* (Geneva: World Council of Churches, n.d.).

[36] Cecil M. Robeck, Jr., *The Assemblies of God and Ecumenical Cooperation*, 1920-1965, Report for Fuller Theological Seminary, Pasadena, California, n.d.

The fourth and final chapter will provide a concise summary and results of this study, and then it will proceed to offer further suggestions based on the results of the study as to how ecumenically minded Christians could more effectively minister to the spiritual and theological concerns of former fundamentalists within the United States. From the conclusions that are reached within this research, the author will proceed to offer recommendations for positive steps that can be taken to affect change, not only among Protestant fundamentalist denominations, but also for the future of ecumenical relations within the 21st century.

Scope and Limitations of this Research

It must be noted that the consultations that will be examined in this study are not specifically conducted by groups that have their origins in the United States, so a significant gap will always be present between the results of the study of the dialogues and the conclusions reached by the author regarding the relationship between former fundamentalists and ecumenical Christians in the United States. However, the author is careful to select dialogues where the theology of the evangelicals closely resembles that of United States fundamentalism, so that relevant connections can be made within the final chapter.

Throughout this research, one has to keep in mind that the former fundamentalist has already abandoned the structure of the previous denomination and is now in the process of embracing a new understanding of Christianity. The process of providing points of comparison and contrast between the theological approaches of two groups-in-question will help the former fundamentalist in the greater process of owning one's belief system and being able to decipher the inconsistencies between the current and former belief systems of the individual as one goes about one's daily life in the United States. In the end, this ongoing process of addressing perceived inconsistencies and questions would promote healing into the life of the former fundamentalist and reintegration into the wider Christian community.

One of the main limitations of this research that has not been addressed is the limitation of time and space that is available to go into case studies, but time does not permit such an endeavor. Since this project will focus a great deal on the doctrine of biblical inerrancy and North American millennial hysteria, which includes "Darbyite Dispensationalism," much emphasis will be placed upon the historical development and theological dimensions of these undeniable elements of United States Protestant fundamentalism.

Another limitation of this research is the generalized references that will be made to United States Protestant fundamentalism. Fundamentalism is a multi-faceted phenomenon that can be found within any religious tradition. In the same way that not all religious fundamentalist groups share the same beliefs and practices, not all Protestant fundamentalist groups in the United States resemble one another in appearances. However, all U.S. Protestant fundamentalist groups share some common features that stem from their common heritage as spiritual descendents of the pietistic immigrants who came over from Europe in search of a newfound freedom in the face of religious tyranny, such as their methods of biblical interpretation and exclusivist natures. The historical background of the United States contributes to an undeniable level of uniformity among the different U.S. fundamentalist groups that ties them together as one overarching form of religious expression. Therefore, this project will focus on U.S. Protestant fundamentalist groups in a generalized manner: as groups with a common heritage and uniform approach to belief and practice, although individual beliefs and practices will differ. While this project will deal with U.S. Protestant fundamentalism in a generalized nature, the next chapter will try to develop a clear historical and cultural basis for U.S. Protestant fundamentalist groups and will narrow in on certain aspects of the greater U.S. fundamentalist movement.

Finally, while the 1993 report *Christian Fundamentalism Today* is a relevant ecumenical document that provides vital information on the global phenomenon of religious fundamentalism, minimal reference will be made to this work within this research. While this document does serve as a catalyst for further speculation on these issues, and consequently, has been an important document for consultation within the beginning stages of this project, it has had no relevant influence upon the conclusions that are presented within the third and fourth chapters of this work. However, this document can provide the reader with a deeper understanding of the distinctive intricacies and challenges of the Christian fundamentalist worldview and experience.

Chapter Two
A Historical Overview of United States Protestant Fundamentalism And A Critical Review of Various American Fundamentalist Movements

Christian fundamentalism can be reduced to one central issue: *biblical inerrancy*.[1] The principal claim of Christian fundamentalism is, "The Bible is divinely inspired and therefore without errors at all...."[2] After making this claim, the Christian fundamentalist will proceed to read the Bible in a variety of ways which correspond to her or his understanding of the Biblical message, which include "...literal as well as non-literal..."[3] methods of interpretation. For the fundamentalist, "Language and world correspond.

---

[1] Kirsten Neilsen, "A Mainline Protestant Perspective," in *Christian Fundamentalism Today*, 40-52:46. The report from WARC, LWF, and PCPCU supplies a quotation from James Barr regarding the issue of biblical inerrancy. According to this report, "Most people would define a fundamentalist way of reading the Bible as a literal reading. But according to Barr 'the point of conflict between fundamentalists and others is not over literality but over inerrancy. What fundamentalists insist is not that the Bible be taken literally, but that it must be interpreted in such a way to avoid any admission that it contains any kind of error'" (46). [James Barr, *Fundamentalism*, London: SCM Press, 1977: 40].
[2] Neilsen, "A Mainline Protestant Perspective" in *Christian Fundamentalism Today*, 46.
[3] *Ibid.*

A Historical Overview of United States Protestant Fundamentalism

A story about a person must be a story about a historical person, who lived and died. And if the biblical texts give different information about the same person, the way out is harmonization. The governing rule remains: no errors in the Bible."[4]

In the United States, this fundamentalist mindset regarding biblical inerrancy can be traced back to the work of Hodge and Warfield, who were both Calvinist professors of Princeton Theological Seminary in the early 1880's. They believed that if God spoke directly through the biblical writers as they were writing: "…their words can be proven to be consistent with known facts in history and science…"[5] However, Hodge and Warfield did acknowledge that the current biblical text is not completely accurate in all of its details, due to countless centuries of copying, but the original documents were completely accurate, as the authors recorded everything which the Holy Spirit dictated to them.[6] According to Hodge and Warfield, one can always rely on the accuracy of the original biblical documents:

> With these presumptions, and in this spirit, let (1) it be proved that each alleged discrepant statement certainly occurred in the original autograph of the sacred book in which it is said to be found. (2) Let it be proved that the interpretation which occasions the apparent discrepancy is the one which the passage was evidently intended to bear. It is not sufficient to show a difficulty, which may spring out of our defective knowledge of the circumstances. The true meaning must be definitely and certainly ascertained, and then shown to be irreconcilable with the other known truth. (3) Let it be proved that the true sense of some part of the original autograph is directly and necessarily inconsistent with some certainly known fact of history, or truth of science, or some other statement of Scripture certainly ascertained and interpreted. We believe that it can be shown that this has never been successfully done in the case of one single alleged instance of error in the WORD OF GOD.[7]

---

[4] *Ibid.*
[5] Gritsch, *Born* Againism, 34.
[6] *Ibid.* Gritsch further refers the reader to Sandeen, *Roots of Fundamentalism*, p. 129, which provides a quotation from the essay "Inspiration" in *Presbyterian Review*, 1881.
[7] Archibald A. Hodge and B.B. Warfield, "Inspiration" in *Presbyterian Review* 2 (1881): 242, cited in Ernest R. Sandeen, *The Roots of Fundamentalism: British and American*

However, even if one believes in the infallibility of the original copies of any religious text, the likelihood is that a time span of thousands of years exists between the moment in which the texts were written and the situation of modern times. Given that one is dealing with an ancient holy text, the culture in which that text was written is so far removed from the culture in which that particular text is interpreted and received. Whenever one adds differences in language and physical environment, the task of deciphering which words of a religious text are truly the words of God becomes extremely difficult, if not impossible. Even if one is able to properly ascribe certain words of a text to God, the question of how to properly apply those words to the present-day context always remains a problem for even the most serious of scholars.

Also, one must remember that whenever dealing with the biblical texts, the problem also presents itself as to which books truly belong to the Christian canon. Certain biblical books that are considered canonical within the Roman Catholic tradition are clearly rejected by Protestant circles. In the same way, the Orthodox Church claims certain books that are rejected by Roman Catholics and Protestants. Whenever one adds the fact that the Jewish tradition, from which Christianity is derived, does not accept the canonicity of the books that Christians label the New Testament, this further complicates the matter of which words within the biblical text are divinely inspired. Given these multiple complications, such a strong statement regarding the inerrancy of the original copies of any religious text does nothing to solve the issue of how to receive those texts today.

It was during the late nineteenth century that many traditional American ideals and customs were being challenged by the developments of modern culture. Some of these developments include, but are not limited to, industrialization, urban poverty, and the arrival of non-Protestant immigrants.[8] Other imminent "threats" to "true" Christianity around the turn of the century included Darwinian evolution, the social gospel, and higher biblical criticism.[9] According to Nancy Ammerman, "Science, technology, and business were taking over where tradition, prayer and

---

Millenarianism, 1800-1930 (Grand Rapids: Baker Book House, 1978), 129. Reference provided by Gritsch, *Born Againism*, 34.

[8] George M. Marsden, *Fundamentalism and American* Culture, 102.

[9] Gritsch, *Born Againism*, 40-41.

faith had left off, streams of European immigrants arriving with Catholic and Jewish traditions, and religious pluralism was becoming a fact of American life."[10]

During this time, certain Protestant religious leaders felt that they had a divine mandate to safeguard the Christian faith for the future generations of America. Consider this statement from a nineteenth century Protestant American minister regarding the constant influx of Roman Catholics into the United States after reading a Baltimore newspaper article reflecting on the proceedings of a nearby Roman Catholic funeral. His rather harsh commentary clearly reflects the anti-Catholic sentiments of many Protestants within nineteenth century North American society:

> Having finished reading the article, I withdrew the paper from my eye and said to myself, Where am I? I thought I was in the United States of America. But that cannot be. This can be no other than Spain, Portugal, or Italy. And what *century* is this? I always thought that I lived in the glorious *nineteenth*. But I must have made a mistake of *nine* at the very least. This surely must be the *tenth* century; the darkest of the dark ages-seculum tenebricosum, as the church historians call it- the *midnight of time! this day* the Prelates- *in this city*-celebrated the solemn office for the *repose, &*c.[11]

It was in response to these perceived threats to the "true" Christian faith that two wealthy Pennsylvanian brothers, Lyman and Milton Stewart, who had received massive fortunes from the oil industry, published a twelve-volume series of pamphlets entitled *The Fundamentals*. *The Fundamentals* were published between 1910 and 1915, and they were freely distributed to every person who worked in any aspect of American religious life. The main topics that were covered in this series were biblical inerrancy, Christian apologetics, and basic Christian doctrines such as the trinity, sin, and substitutionary atonement. *The Fundamentals* also addressed

---

[10] Nancy Ammerman, Source Unknown in "Visit Sullivan County, Tennessee: Christian Fundamentalism Exposed," via *Internet*, Web Page Updated February 12, 2003: <http://www.sullivan-county.com/news/>. Accessed March 1, 2005.
[11] Rev. William Nevins, D.D., "Thoughts on Popery"(158-159) in *Nevins Practical Thoughts. & Popery*, Evangelical Family Library, printer D. Fanshaw (New York: The American Tract Society, 1836).

the relationship between religion and science, and it contained a section that attacked other contemporaneous belief systems, such as Roman Catholicism, Mormonism, and Christian Science.[12]

It was through this document that the fundamentalist movement received its name: "When in 1920 the term 'fundamentalist' was coined, it called to mind the broad united front of the kind of opposition to modernism that characterized these widely known."[13] In the 1920's, the fundamentalist movement adopted the five basic doctrines of the 1910 Presbyterian General Assembly, which served to clarify the theological boundaries of the fundamentalist belief system. These five points included: (1) biblical inerrancy, (2) the actuality of the virgin birth, (3) substitutionary atonement, (4) the literal bodily resurrection of Jesus, and (5) the empirical reality of the miracles of Jesus.[14]

While these five fundamentalist principles were originally coined as an evangelical front to combat the empirical claims of modern science, the striking reality is that the fundamentalists borrowed them from among the interpretive categories of modern science in order to make such objective claims regarding the empirical validity of certain biblical events. It must be noted that the categories of empiricism and objectivity are modern scientific constructs that are foreign to the philosophical worldview of the ancient world. In making such empirical claims about certain biblical events, the fundamentalists of the early 1920's ruled out any possibilities of other possible methods of interpretation of these biblical narratives, such as a symbolic approach. In the same way, the claim that the doctrine of substitutionary atonement- the idea that the death of Jesus atoned for the sins or shortcomings of humanity- is the only possible way to interpret the biblical narrative does not leave room for other methods of appropriating the message of the cross within Christianity.[15]

---

[12] Richard Flory, "Fundamentals, The" in *Encyclopedia of Fundamentalism*, Religion & Society: A Berkshire Reference Book, ed. Brenda E. Brasher (New York/London: Routledge, 2001), 186-188: 186.

[13] Mardsen, *Fundamentalism and American Culture*, 119.

[14] Ibid., 117.

[15] For further information on this topic, see Joel B. Green and Mark Baker, *Recovering the Scandal of the Cross: Atonement in New Testament and Contemporary Contexts* (Illinois: Intervarsity Press, 2000). Green and Baker argue throughout this text that the model of substitutionary atonement is based on legal categories that are specific to the context of the Western world.

John Nelson Darby: The Father of Modern Dispensationalism

John Nelson Darby is popularly regarded as the "Father of Modern Dispensationalism," which is an American religious apocalyptic movement that surfaced around the middle to the end of the nineteenth century and continues to be widely accepted among Christian fundamentalist groups. Dispensationalism attempts to divide prophetic history into a predetermined number of periods, which are called dispensations.[16] During each dispensation, "…God offers humankind a beneficent covenantal relationship, with faith and obedience the proper response. The immediate and inevitable failure of humanity to react appropriately to this divine generosity promptly condemns it anew."[17]

Darby was an Anglo-Irish clergyman who was ordained as an Anglican priest. However, he was convinced that the church hierarchy, and the visible church in general, was corrupt, and as a result of these sentiments, he renounced his ordination and developed a following of like-minded individuals, which was called the Plymouth Brethren. Darby traveled frequently to the United States in order to preach his message, and his message spread rapidly among many new settlers.[18]

Based on the simple-minded hermeneutical method of biblical literalism, "…which required that the Bible be understood solely in terms of the plain, grammatical meaning of its language,"[19] Darby taught that

---

Furthermore, one must note that whenever the doctrine of substitutionary atonement is coupled with the doctrine of the Trinity-the idea that the Father, Son (Jesus), and the Holy Spirit are three entities in one- one must ask the question as to how the death of Jesus can bridge the gap which exists between a perfect deity and sinful humanity, if no intrinsic connection exists between humanity and God in the first place. For the author of this research project, this is the problem that presented itself whenever it came to the fundamentalist claim that the atoning death of Jesus provides reconciliation between God and humanity. Of course, countless other problems present themselves within the doctrine of substitutionary atonement, but the author does not have the time or space to address all of them or to go into further detail on the other doctrines which are referred to within this section.

[16] Robert K. Whalen, "Dispensationalism" in Encyclopedia of Millenialism and Millennial Movements. Religion and Society: A Berkshire Reference Work, ed. Richard A. Landes (New York/London: Routledge, 2000), 125-128: 125.

[17] Ibid., 126.

[18] Ibid., 126.

[19] *Ibid*. This was literalism according to the Anglo-Saxon grammatical structure with little to no regard for the original languages of the text.

Jesus could secretly return at any moment (the event commonly known as the "rapture") to gather the "true" spiritual church from this present evil world. His theory is based on I Thessalonians 4:16-17, where it states that the dead in Christ shall rise first, and then all those who are alive will be caught up with Jesus in the air. Shortly after this occurrence, a period of intense worldwide tribulation will take place, where there will be unparalleled suffering under the power of Satan and the Antichrist. At the end of this period, Satan will be banished from the earth, and Jesus will return with his saints and establish the millennial kingdom in Jerusalem.[20] This second appearing of Jesus is known as the "Second Advent," which Darby claimed could be found in Matthew 24.[21] In this passage, the disciples are asking about the signs that will accompany the end of the age, and Jesus responds by predicting a time of tribulation that will precede the coming of the "Son of Man."[22]

Many sincere fundamentalists and evangelicals link these two passages together in order to provide a biblical basis for the doctrine of a pre-tribulation rapture. These Christians are aware that Jesus speaks of a time of great troubles in Matthew, but in this particular text, Jesus mentions nothing about anyone being taken into heaven prior to this occurrence. In fact, he states quite the opposite.[23] Furthermore, I Thessalonians 4:16-17

---

[20] Whalen, "Dispensationalism" in *EMMM*, 127.
[21] Sandeen, *The Roots of Fundamentalism*, 63.
[22] See Matthew 24:29-31.
[23] For further analysis on this time of unparalleled troubles, see Ulrich Luz, *New Testament Theology: The Theology of the Gospel of Matthew*, eds. James D.G. Dunn et al, trans. J. Bradford Robinson (Great Britain: Cambridge University Press, 1993), 126. Luz argues that the author of Matthew, who was writing after the destruction of the Temple in 70 A.D., is actually using the story of the conversation between Jesus and his disciples to remind the reader of events that have already taken place. Luz writes, "The wars mentioned in verses 6-8 are probably the events that occurred around the years 66 to 70AD, now viewed from a cosmopolitan standpoint. We need only to think of 68 AD, the Year of the Three Caesars, when 'nation made war upon nation, and kingdom upon kingdom'. Matthew applies to these events the apocalyptic 'birth pang'. In other words, they are an omen foreshadowing the end of time, but are not the end itself" (127). Luz also adds that verses 15-22, which refer to the prophecies of Daniel are a "backward glance" at the Jewish War; (it is unclear to which war he is referring, but most likely to the Maccabbean Revolt-refer ahead to pp. 24-25 for information surrounding this event) of which the timing has already been "cut short" for the sake of the "elect," and at any time, the end could come. Therefore, as Luz concludes, Matthew 24 is not meant to be

A Historical Overview of United States Protestant Fundamentalism

is referring to the end-time event of the resurrection when "…the living and the dead are united to be forever with one another and with the Lord."[24] These particular verses are in response to those people who were awaiting the imminent return of Christ and rightfully wondered what would happen to their loved ones in Christ who had already died. This is why Paul ends this chapter with "Therefore, comfort one another with these words" (I Thess. 4:18 *RSV*).[25] This passage mentions nothing of a secret "snatching away" of Christians while everyone else is left on earth to suffer before the coming of the Christ. However, many pre-tribulation fundamentalists will claim that just as Noah was protected from the flood, God will protect Christians from the time of great persecution, and they will proceed to invoke I Thessalonians 4:16-17 in attempt to substantiate this argument.

Once again, this is another example of a contextual reading of the scriptures-in-question. Darby is clearly frustrated with the established religion in Ireland, and he is seeking a messianic era in which these struggles will end. It is highly possible that he draws some unconscious parallels in his mind between the supposed rapture of the church and the great escape of many Christians to the New World. His preaching excursions in America testified to the fact that he most likely saw America as part of this messianic plan, and he wanted as many Americans as possible to take part in this unparalleled moment on the eschatological timetable.

In 1909, Cyrus I. Scofield, a prominent American attorney who was attracted to the dispensationalist theories of Darby, carefully inserted his (Scofield's) own dispensationalist notes into the popular *Scofield Reference Bible*,[26] which is still used widely by many modern fundamentalists. Through

---

read chronologically, but given the addition of the parables at the end; one can conclude, "…their main purpose is to warn." (128). However, the author of this research believes that given the non-chronological layout of this chapter, the author of Matthew could be implying the cyclical nature of such events as they are played out in history and lead to new levels of cosmic transformation, much in the same way that the birth of a new child follows the "birth pangs," and this birthing process makes way for a new cycle of birthing to begin. (Note: Luz refers the reader to other authors who provide further commentary on these issues as well).

[24] H. Rolston, *Thessalonians to Philemon*. The Layman's Bible Commentaries (London: SCM Press Ltd. 1963), 33.
[25] Ibid., 34.
[26] Whalen, "Dispensationalism" in *EMMM*, 128.

his work, Scofield sought to present the Bible from the perspective, that at any time, this present dispensation could end, and the rapture could occur. He provided extensive notes and cross references throughout the Bible supporting this theory.[27] Unfortunately, many sincere readers of the *Scofield Reference Bible* "…have been unaware of the distinction between the ancient text and the Scofield interpretation."[28] Within his work, Scofield identifies seven separate dispensations in which God deals differently with God's people, which have been listed by Gritsch:

> Two concerns dominate Scofield's millennialism: to understand all of human history in terms of ages or dispensations which close the history of salvation, climaxing in the advent of the millennium, and to distinguish between Christians and Jews. Accordingly, there are seven dispensations: (1) the age of innocence, the covenant between God and Adam in Eden; (2) the age of conscience, the covenant between God and Adam after the Fall; (3) the age of human government, the covenant between God and Noah after the Flood; (4) the age of promise, the covenant between God and Abraham, in whom Israel is chosen; (5) the age of the law, the covenant between God and Moses, ending with the crucifixion of Jesus by Jews and Gentiles; (6) the age of grace, the covenant in and through Jesus for individual Jews and Gentiles until the Second Coming of Christ; and (7) the age of the fulness of time, the millennium of Christ, and the restoration of the Davidian kingdom.[29]

Around the turn of the century, there was a general level of hysteria surrounding the secret return of Jesus to claim his people. Reverend George E. Guille, who was a professor at Moody Bible Institute, spoke of the moment when the last person on some remote island would usher in the end of this present dispensation by accepting the Gospel message.[30]

---

[27] Sandeen, *The Roots of Fundamentalism*, 222
[28] *Ibid.*
[29] Gritsch, *Born Againism*, 21.
[30] Reference made to *Coming and Kingdom of Christ* (Chicago, 1914), 183, in Sandeen, *The Roots of Fundamentalism*, 226. Sandeen provides a quotation from Guille: "'The last member of that bride, may, from some remote island of the sea, be called out during this hour in which we are together, and, immediately, the nedt event in God's program will transpire. It will be…the descent of the Lord into the air, and the rapture of the saints to meet Him there.'"

A Historical Overview of United States Protestant Fundamentalism

This belief was based on a strict Calvinistic understanding that only God knows the number of people who will experience salvation during this age of grace, or the Church Age, as fundamentalists commonly call it. Such frenzy even presented itself at the 1884 Niagara Conference on dispensationalist prophecy, where the delegates would ring the bell at the break of dawn to remind everyone to stand ready, because the rapture could occur at any moment.[31]

The Millerites: An Earlier Example of U.S. Millennial Obsession

The emergence of "Darbyite Dispensationalism" is not the first outbreak of millennial obsession to surface in United States history. Earlier in 1816, an American man by the name of William Miller had a personal conversion experience that compelled him to study the scriptures for two years. During this time, he became obsessed with predicting what he saw as the imminent return of Christ. He derived his method of date setting from Daniel 8-9.[32] One can reach this conclusion based on these biblical passages that Miller's prediction was taken from Daniel 9: 24-27:

> 'Seventy weeks of years are decreed concerning your people and your holy city, to finish the transgression, to put an end to sin, and to atone for iniquity, to bring in everlasting righteousness, to seal both vision and prophet and to anoint a most high place. Know therefore and understand that from the going forth of the word to restore and build Jerusalem to the coming of an anointed one, a prince, there shall be seven weeks. Then for sixty-two weeks it shall be built again with squares and moat, but in a trouble time. And after the sixty-two weeks, an anointed one shall be cut off, and shall have nothing; and the people of the prince who is to come shall destroy the city and the sanctuary. Its end shall come with a flood, and to the end there shall be war; desolations are decreed. And he shall make a strong covenant with many for one week; and for

---

[31] Gritsch, *Born Againism*, 37.
[32] Author Unknown, "Millerites" in "Apologetics Index" (research resource), ed. Anton Hein, via *Internet* (August 23, 2004): <http://apologeticsindex.org/m10.html>. Accessed March 19, 2005.

half of the week he shall cause sacrifice and offering to cease; and upon the wing of abominations shall come one who makes desolate, until the decreed end is poured out on the desolator' (*RSV*).

Miller calculated 2300 years from the date that Ezra was given permission to rebuild the Temple, which Miller identified as 457 BCE. Given his calculations, he predicted that the end of this age would occur sometime during the period between March 21, 1843 and March 21, 1844.[33] When his prediction did not come true, he admitted that he had miscalculated, and he reset the date as October 22, 1844. Miller's error of judgment is popularly known as the "Great Disappointment," because nearly 50,000 people believed his teachings, only to find out that his predictions were in error. After his predictions did not come true, many disenchanted followers abandoned his teachings. However, many remained and became the spiritual progenitors of the modern Seventh-day Adventists and the Davidian-Seventh-Day Adventists, of which the widely publicized Branch Davidian cult of Waco, Texas was a tragic offshoot.[34]

Unfortunately, history shows that many well-meaning people who have attempted to make apocalyptic predictions have caused much heartache. Miller, a newly converted Christian who was not a biblical scholar, took the task of intense biblical study upon himself with only the Protestant version of the Christian scriptures at his disposal. Therefore, he had no contact with the deuterocanonical and apocryphal texts,[35] which are

---

[33] For information on William Miller, see also Editor(s) Unknown, World Council of Churches, "The Church, The Churches and The World Council of Churches: The Ecclesiological Significance of the World Council of Churches" in *So Much In Common: Documents of Interest in the Conversations Between the World Council of Churches and the Seventh-day Adventist Church* (Geneva: World Council of Churches, 1973), 47-68: 65-66. Regarding the calculations of Miller, *So Much in Common* states: "According to their reading of Daniel 8 and 9 the 2,300 days mentioned there signify the same number of years; these began in 457 B.C. with an initial period of 70 weeks of years (490 years) which lasted until 31/2 years after the death of Christ (who was crucified in the middle of the last 'week' of years). Therefore the date upon which the 'cleansing of the heavenly sanctuary' would begin, on this basis of calculation, is 1844 (i.e. 2,3000 years after 457 B.C., 1810 years after the last of the 70 weeks of years)" (66).

[34] "Millerites" in "Apologetic Index," ed. Hein, via *Internet*: <http://www.apologeticsindex.org/m10.html>.

[35] The reference to deuterocanonical and apocryphal texts refers to books that are, as well as those that are not, regarded as canonical within the Eastern Orthodox and Roman

essential components to an in-depth study of the apocalyptic predictions of Daniel.

Miller interpreted the prophecies of Daniel in light of the death of Jesus, but in doing so, he is overlooking many key events in the history of Israel, which are recorded in the apocalyptic literature of the deuterocanonical books such as the Maccabees, the Wisdom of Solomon, Tobit, Judith, the apocryphal Enoch, and many other books.[36] D.S. Russell comments, "In Daniel 9.25, 26 we read of 'an anointed one, a prince' and of another 'anointed one (who) shall be cut off', the references being presumably to the High Priests Jeshua and Onias III, respectively."[37] This chapter, which must have been written at a time much later than that of Daniel,[38] reflects back to the time just prior to the Maccabean Revolt, when Jeshua (Greek: Jason), due to the help of a bribe, replaced the legitimate High Priest Onias III as a political move to Hellenize the Jewish people during a time when the Jews underwent intense persecution.[39] Furthermore, the reference to "weeks" is a common symbolic element of apocalyptic literature.[40] It is not a literal statement concerning chronological time, as time is often understood in the West.

Catholic traditions, but are rejected by Protestants. Apocryphal texts are specifically forbidden, whereas deuterocanonical texts are included within the canon.

[36] D.S. Russell, *Between the Testaments* (London: SCM Press Ltd., 1960), 122.

[37] *Ibid.*

[38] See John J. Collins, *Daniel: A Commentary on the Book of Daniel* (with an Essay "The Influence of Daniel on the New Testament," by Adela Yarbro Collins) Hermeneia/ A Critical and Historical Commentary on the Bible, ed. Frank Moore Cross (Minneapolis: Fortress Press, 1993), 347. It is argued that the beginning prayer of Daniel in chapter nine is a later redaction to the rest of the chapter, which "…flows smoothly, full of traditional phrases and free of Aramaisms, and it contrasts sharply with the difficult Hebrew that is characteristic of Daniel" (347). (See also Collins' footnotes for more references on this topic). When the further contents of this chapter are compared with the events in the history of Israel during Hellenistic times, they add credibility to the belief that this chapter was written much later than during the time of the Babylonian captivity.

[39] Russell, *Between the Testaments*, 26-27.

[40] John J. Collins, *Daniel*, 353.

The Prophecies of Ellen G. White: The Continuation of Millerite Apocalypticism

Ellen G. White was a devotee of Miller who claimed to see many visions of heaven and the end of this present age. White reported seeing visions as early as seventeen years old, and although she was never ordained or proclaimed an official leader within the Millerite movement, she was greatly revered by many Adventists. She never made infallible claims concerning her visions; nevertheless many people took her visions so seriously that the Adventist movement has been accused of not being a biblically based denomination.[41]

Around the same time that White reported her visions, many Christians accused her of being a follower of Spiritualism, which was a popular form of spirituality in which practitioners claimed to have had encounters with the world beyond. She was so concerned about these accusations that she devoted one of the chapters of her writings to refuting Spiritualism,[42] and more importantly, the popular practice of "table rapping," through which the practitioner would communicate messages to the spirit world and listen for its reply in the form of rapping noises on the table. White attributed the practice of table rapping to the devil and his minions, while she claimed that Jesus himself had appeared in her visions.[43]

The visions of White were based on a dualistic conception of reality, drawing sharp contrasts between those who are the true followers of Jesus and those who are followers of darkness. In her visions, a large group of people begins to follow Jesus, but along the way, many become discouraged and drop away from the following.[44] White concludes that these people

---

[41] WCC, "The Church" in *So Much In Common*, 59-60. The author(s) refer the reader to Le Roy Edwin Froom, *The Prophetic Faith of Our Fathers*, vol. IV (Washington D.C., Review and Herald Publishing Association, 1954), 976 ff. A number of other relevant resources within these pages are also referenced.

[42] Ellen G. White, "Mysterious Rapping" in "Ellen White's Early Writings" (Full Text Writings of Ellen G. White Provided by the Trustees of the Ellen G. White Publications, Washington, D.C., 1963), 59-61, via *Internet*: <http://english.sdaglobal.org/dnl/books/images/ew.htm#20>: HostMaster: SDA Global:<hitechgroup@rogers.com>. Accessed March 20, 2005.

[43] White, "The Gathering Time" in "Early Writings," 74-78: 77, via *Internet*. See above address.

[44] White, "My First Vision" in "Early Writings," 13-31: 15, via *Internet*. Written by White shortly after the "Great Disappointment"-1844. Shortly after Miller's predictions did not come true, many people left the movement. "My First Vision" was published in 1846.

were never truly children of God by alluding to the possibility that they were predestined from the beginning to fall into eternal damnation. Of those who eventually fall away from the "true" fold, White writes, "Others rashly denied the light behind them and said that it was not God that had led them out so far. The light behind them went out, leaving their feet in perfect darkness, and they stumbled and lost sight of the mark and of Jesus, and fell off the path down into the dark and wicked world below."[45] Of the elect, White continues, "The living saints, 144,000 in number, knew and understood the voice, while the wicked people thought it was thunder and earthquake."[46] The content of these visions undoubtedly reflects the natural progression of the Millerite movement, in which many early devotees did not remain committed to the Adventist cause. Such occurrences most likely had some level of influence on the content of her visions and upon her worldview.

The Born-Again Movement: A Conservative Reaction Against Theological Liberalism

After the rise of rationalism, social progress and optimism in the 1920's, against which many fundamentalists reacted, the ever-increasing gap between theological conservatives and liberals in the United States became much more apparent as time progressed. Many evangelicals and fundamentalists criticized the way that the Protestant churches in the United States had embraced theological liberalism, due to the increasing influence of rationalism, scientific empiricism, and consequently, higher biblical criticism, on the American scene. In reaction to this phenomenon, they cried out for more emphasis to be placed on the evangelization of souls rather than on improving the material conditions of humankind.[47]

Much like the revival preachers that preceded them, these vibrant evangelical voices could not have overemphasized the role of personal faith in the atoning death of Jesus, which is also referred to as the experience of

---

[45] *Ibid.*
[46] *Ibid.*
[47] Lee E. Dirks, *Religion in Action: How America's Faiths are Meeting New Challenges.* Newsbook (Silver Springs, Maryland: The National Observer, 1965), 156.

being "Born Again." One author quotes the popular American evangelist Billy Graham, a North Carolina native, as having said, "'You must turn to Christ by simple faith and accept Him as your Lord and Savior.' A pause. 'Notice again, I said, 'by faith.'"[48] The need for a simplistic faith was seen as a welcome contradiction to the seemingly more ambiguous message of more liberal mainline Protestant churches, which were more social gospel oriented, partially due to the influence of higher biblical criticism.

Even as early as the mid-1800's, many theologically conservative leaders, such as William Miller, were decrying the German higher biblical criticism that was making its way into countless divinity schools across America. Many of these lay ministers foresaw the emerging developments of modernity within American culture as imminent threats to the simplicity of the gospel message. Like the Reformers in Europe who questioned the sole authority of religious officials to interpret the scriptures for the people, these American lay religious leaders advocated the rights of average church members and divinity students to interpret the scriptures for themselves.[49] William Miller, in speaking of theological education in the States, is quoted as having said:

> is always founded on some sectarian creed. It may do to take a blank mind and impress it with this kind, but it will always end in bigotry. A free mind will never be satisfied with the views of others. Were I a teacher of youth of divinity, I would first learn their capacity, and mind. If these were good, I would make them study bible for themselves, and send them out free to do the world good. But if they had no mind I would stamp them with another's mind, write bigot on their forehead, and send them out as slaves.[50]

---

[48] *Ibid.* Dirks is quoting from Billy Graham as he preached at the Billy Graham Pavilion at the World's Fair in California (see p. 156). The exact date of this message is unspecified by the author, but it is clear that this occurred sometime prior to 1965, given the publication date of this book. According to David Harrell, Billy Graham gained national recognition during the conservative 1950's. [David Edwin Harrell, "Billy Graham" in *Christianity in America: A Handbook*, A Lion Book, eds. Mark A. Noll, et al (Grand Rapids: William B. Eerdmans Publishing Company, 1983), 435-437: 436.].

[49] Author(s) Unknown, "Theology and Religious Belief" in *Christianity in America*, ed. Noll, 221-233: 223.

[50] William Miller quoted in *Ibid.* The author does not specify from where this quotation is derived. The author of this chapter follows the quotation of Miller with this striking

A Historical Overview of United States Protestant Fundamentalism

From the Born-Again Theology of Billy Graham to the 1970's Charismatic Movement

When examining the theology of Billy Graham, who rose to fame during the 1950's,[51] one cannot ignore the impact that the historical developments of the time had on his simplistic approach to the gospel. The United States had just endured the horrific era of the Second World War, and consequently, the American public was seeking a simplistic lifestyle that provided quick answers to many tough questions concerning the limits of human potential and the capability of humankind to destroy itself. There was also a growing fear of Communism.[52] During this time, many American families sought simplistic lifestyles with the nuclear family as the standard model for American family life. There was also a great emphasis placed on the woman reclaiming her "rightful" role in the home as devoted wife and mother after her return from aiding in the war effort. The fifties is the decade during which the proverbial saying "a little house with a white picket fence" came into vogue. For many Americans, the simplicity of family and community life replaced the unbearable complexities of the greater world scene. Therefore, it should not come as a surprise that many modern fundamentalists often refer to the lifestyle of the 1950's with unprecedented nostalgia.

However, this conservative mentality was shaken during the turbulent 1960's with the assassination of President John F. Kennedy, and the Civil Rights Movement, and most importantly, the Vietnam War. All of a sudden, the secure family lifestyle that was created during the 1950's was being shaken by the Vietnam War draft. Countless young people, many of who were eligible for the military draft, participated in open protests, and many young men dodged the draft. Countless protestors during this time engaged in licentious behaviors, which included free sex and the use of hallucinogenic drugs. This was the same timeframe in which the highly romanticized "Woodstock" music festival occurred. Many young people also escaped the horrors of the modern society to find refuge in communes. During this period, "Eastern mysticism, new forms of self-awareness, and

---

comment: "In this climate, it is no wonder that American clergymen were given to restructuring theology for popular consumption" (see page 223).
[51] Refer back to footnote 80: Harrell, "Billy Graham" in *Christianity in America*, 436.

spiritual narcissism became popular."[53] During this decade, many people challenged the objective authorities of all established power structures, such as church and state.

After the turbulence of this era reached its culmination, the many of the former "hippies," as they are commonly called, "…became disillusioned with the 'new spirituality' and its psychedelic trappings. A significant segment of the youth culture was ripe for a return to old-time religion."[54] However, many former drug addicts, who at the same time craved and rejected the sense of stability that can be found in traditional forms of religious expression, turned to a new form of religious expression, which combined key elements, the "old-time religion" of their childhoods and the tempestuous experiences that followed life within the youth counterculture. This religious movement was popularly labeled the "Jesus Movement," and the groups within this movement "…were characterized by a kind of grass-roots diversity manifested in widely scattered subgroups which lacked a single leadership structure and clear-cut goals and objectives."[55] Followers of this movement were often referred to as "Jesus freaks,"[56] and they could be seen engaging in mass baptisms in the Pacific Ocean of California[57] and repeating popular slogans, such as, "'You're in the Rapture Generation' and 'The Bible is Soul Food.'"[58]

As with most religious movements this movement eventually crystallized in the modern-day Charismatic Movement: an offshoot of Pentecostalism characterized by a strong evangelistic fervor and a seeking after the "gifts of the Spirit." It was during this same timeframe that many evangelical campus groups, such as Campus Crusade for Christ and InterVarsity

---

[52] In the early 1950's, Billy Graham wrote, "Materialism, Communism, and all the other philosophical interpretations do not hold a candle to what Christ offers." [Billy Graham, *Peace With God* (Garden City, New York: Doubleday and Company, Inc., 1953), 217.). This statement by Billy Graham is characteristic of how evangelical religion was used in the United States during the 1950's to counter the supposed threats of Communism.

[53] Ronald M. Enroth, "The Christian Counterculture" in *Christianity in America*, 469-470: 469.

[54] *Ibid.*

[55] *Ibid.*

[56] Ibid., 470.

[57] See photo on 470: *Christianity in America*.

[58] Ibid., 470.

Fellowship, gained popularity among college students.[59] Therefore, when Jimmy Carter, an avowed evangelical and devout Southern Baptist Sunday School teacher, was elected as President of the United States, "…1976, was quickly declared to be 'the Year of the Evangelical.'"[60]

The Doomsday Prophets of the 1970's: From Books to Films

However, the excitement surrounding the new evangelical President did not last, because many people concluded, "…that the President was, no matter what he said on TV, a big fat crook…."[61] Therefore, many segments of American culture, including the speeches of many politicians and many science fiction films, projected this dire attitude towards the future. Many Americans also began to fear for the condition of the environment, with great concern for the harm that pollution was doing to the seas and the Ozone Layer.[62] Also, there continued to be general mistrust for the government in general as gas prices continued to rise. The entire decade of the 1970's was also a time in which the fear of Communist takeover of the United States gained heightened attention. According to one source: "The government was trying to quell food riots and planning to issue 'red money,' worth one-half the value of the green stuff."[63] Consequently, many American evangelicals strongly felt that the return of Jesus was just on the horizon. Once again, apocalyptic hysteria began to resurface on the American frontier.

The act of predicting the eventual takeover of Communism became a full-time occupation for many of the doomsday prophets of the early 1970's. One such doomsday prophet was Hal Lindsey, a campus preacher

---

[59] Author(s) Unknown, "An Unruly Time (1960-1980)" in *Christianity in America*, 449-489: 471.
[60] *Ibid.*
[61] Author(s) Unknown, "End Times Movies, Pt. II: Take the Mark" Article first appeared in the online magazine *The Control Voice*" Sponsor: Adult Christianity, via *Internet*: (Hurricane Electronic Internet Services, 1995-2004.): <http://www.jesus21/content/movies/rapture2.html>: Accessed April 7, 2005.
[62] "End Time Movies," via *Internet:* <http://www.jesus21/content/movies/rapture2.html>.
[63] *Ibid.*

based out of Southern California, who published the popular prophetic thriller novel: *The Late Great Planet Earth* [64] in 1970, which is based on Darbyite Dispensationalism.[65] Paul Boyer, Professor of History from the University of Wisconsin comments, "Theologically there is nothing new there. What he does is link it to current events: the Cold War, nuclear war, the Chinese communist threat, the restoration of Israel. All of these events, he links to specific biblical passages in the classical fashion of prophecy popularizers."[66]

Two years later, Lindsey publishes his second book: *Satan is Alive and Well on Planet Earth*, [67] which also gained much attention from evangelical and fundamentalist circles. This work attributes the various trends within modern culture to the work of Satan. Lindsey warns readers about the possible dangers of certain types of popular music and movies, which subtly prepare the world for the eventual reign of the Antichrist. Of television programs, Lindsey unapologetically writes, "From cartoons to comedy, the mind benders use the television controls to channel us into the mold of the world system." [68] Lindsey also spends a great deal of time decrying spiritualism, astrology, and other psychic phenomena,[69] while

---

[64] Hal Lindsey, *The Late Great Planet Earth*, with C.C. Carlson (Grand Rapids, Michigan: Zondervan, 1970).

[65] Paul Boyer, "Apocalypticism Explained: America's Doomsday Industry" article in "Apocalypse! The Evolution of Apocalyptic Belief and How it Shaped the Western World," PBS: Frontline, producer WGBH Boston (November 1999): via *Internet*: <http://pbs.org/wgbh/pages/frontline/shows/apocalypse/>. Accessed April 10, 2005.

[66] Paul Boyer, "Apocalypticism Explained: America's Doomsday Industry" article in "Apocalypse! The Evolution of Apocalyptic Belief and How it Shaped the Western World," via *Internet*: <http://pbs.org/wgbh/pages/frontline/shows/apocalypse/>.

[67] Hal Lindsey, *Satan is Alive and Well on Planet Earth* with C.C. Carlson (Grand Rapids, Michigan: Zondervan Publishing House, 1972).

[68] Ibid., 109.

[69] Ibid., 39. One chapter entitled "Angels of Light" is devoted exclusively to the psychic Jeane Dixon (pp. 114-128). The attitude of Lindsey is not too far removed from that of Ellen G. White, acclaimed prophetess of the Millerites, who was accused of practicing spiritualism and expended much energy on refuting the charges. It should be noted that Lindsey himself sends contradictory messages when he deals with such issues. He makes reference to a girl of whom he accused of being "…under the influence of an evil spirit" (p. 17); this girl happened to have been wearing a Scottish kilt that ironically contained his family plaid. The girl told Lindsey, " 'A few weeks ago I was in Scotland. While I was there, I had a premonition that I was going to meet someone named Lindsey and that

A Historical Overview of United States Protestant Fundamentalism

adding his own commentary on the issue: "I believe that people are being given superhuman powers from Satan in order that they may promote his work on earth."[70]

During the same year that Lindsey's second book was published, Mark IV Productions, which was based out of Des Moines, Iowa, produced the first of a four-part low budget film series based on the dispensationalist theology of John Nelson Darby. This first film was entitled *A Thief in the Night*,[71] and it portrays life after the rapture. It features a young woman by the name of Patty Myers (played by Patty Dunning), who dreams that she wakes up one morning to find that her recently converted husband has just disappeared in the rapture. Since the disappearance of so many Christians produced a worldwide catastrophe, the world comes together under one government: the government of the Antichrist, which requires all citizens to either take the "mark of the beast," a mark placed on the right hand or forehead that condemns one to eternal damnation, or be subsequently imprisoned and beheaded. Patty, who is reluctant of taking the mark due to the influence of Christian friends prior to the rapture, is simultaneously uncertain about her decision to become a Christian. Therefore, she spends the entire movie running away from the one-world government, which is called UNITE (the United Nations Imperium for Total Emergency). Towards the end of the movie, she wakes up to find that it was all just a dream. However, now the worst is yet to come, as she finds her husband's buzzing razor in the bathroom sink.[72]

---

he would have a profound effect on my life. That is the reason I bought the plaid kilt." (p. 165-166). Like White, he attributes this premonition to the work of Jesus, when ordinarily; he would have attributed such a premonition to the work of the devil.

[70] Ibid., 40.

[71] Mark IV Productions, *A Thief in the Night*. Director Donald W. Thompson. Writing Credits: Russell S. Doughten, Jr., and Jim Grant (Des Moines, Iowa: 1972). Author's Note: One should be careful to take note of the countless subtle and unsubtle references to Communism made within this film. This film is very reflective of the times in which it was produced.

[72] Author Unknown, "End Time Movies," via *Internet:* <http://jesus21.com/content/movies/rapture2.html>: A Movie Review. The author writes, "The film opens with menacing scripture over the menacing sound of a ticking clock. It's Patty's clock, and she wakes up to a radio blaring quotes from scripture. (This is a motif in all the Mark IV rapture films: whenever anything prophetically significant occurs, it's explained by newscasters, awkwardly)…then Patty wakes up **again** and it was all a dream. (Bet you

The three other films in this series include: *A Distant Thunder* (1977),[73] *Image of the Beast* (1981),[74] and *The Prodigal Planet* (1983).[75] In spite of the fact that these films reflect the aforementioned incoherent apocalyptic theology of John Nelson Darby, and that the content of these movies largely reflect the prevalent fear of Communism during the 1970's and the 1980's, many fundamentalist groups have used, and still continue to use, these films for the sole purpose of scaring people into becoming Christians. The author of this research can testify to this reality firsthand, as her sixth grade class was forced to watch this film series in a small private fundamentalist school during the early 1990's. Later, a youth group leader in her church showed the first film to a particular class in her church. As the author has browsed the *Internet*, she found many testimonies that clarify her theories surrounding the traumas that these films perpetrate. Referring to the first movie in the series, one such film critic comments:

> I saw this movie when I was about ten years old. I had nightmares about it for years. It, along with many other bad experiences, served to define my opinion of Christianity as an adult. Until recently, the evangelical Christians were a tolerable nuisance in daily life. But movies like this serve to underscore the politics of fear used by the right to scare people into compliance and conformity. Hopefully, in the thirty two years that have passed since this movie came out, those of us who have learned to resist propaganda can watch something like this as a study in camp rather than a serious statement about a 'loving' religion. AND DON'T LET CHILDREN WATCH THIS!![76]

---

can't see what's coming.) Then it starts all over again, the clock, the radio, the razor and Patty collapses by her bed and just screams and screams and screams."

[73] Mark IV Productions, *A Distant Thunder*. Director Donald W. Thompson. Screenplay and Story: Russell S. Doughten, Jr. (Des Moines, Iowa: 1977).

[74] Mark IV Productions, *Image of the Beast*. Director Donald W. Thompson. Writing Credits: Russell S. Doughten, Jr. and Donald W. Thompson (Des Moines, Iowa: 1981).

[75] Mark IV Productions, *The Prodigal Planet*. Director Donald W. Thompson. Screenplay and Story: Russell S. Doughten, Jr. (Des Moines, Iowa: 1983).

[76] Snarky One, Seattle "Right Wing Extremist Propaganda" (IMDb User Comments for *A Thief in the Night* (1972): November 12, 2004), via *Internet*: <http://www.imdb.com/title/tt0070795/#comment>. Accessed April 10, 2005.

The 1980's: The Decade of the New Religious Right

As the apocalyptic frenzy of the seventies eventually subsided, and the doomsday prophets became increasingly comfortable with their surroundings this side of the rapture, they concluded that while they were still present on earth, they felt that they had been given a mandate by God to claim their rightful roles as Christian witnesses in American society. Therefore, the New Christian Right, which is the Christian branch of the New Religious Right,[77] began emerging into different sectors of the political arena. Wilcox defines the New Christian Right as "...a social movement that attempts to mobilize evangelical Protestants and other orthodox Christians into conservative political action."[78]

The development of the New Right can be traced back to 1979, when the Moral Majority was formed.[79] The Moral Majority reflects a 1950's view of society and the role of the family; it stands for the integrity of the nuclear family and opposes feminism, abortion, divorce, and homosexuality. Some of its prominent figureheads include Jerry Falwell, Beverly LaHaye, and James Dobson. After the election of President Ronald Reagan in 1980, various Moral Majority leaders entered public office, such as Bob Billings, who served on the Department of Education, and C. Everett Koop, who was appointed by Reagan as Surgeon General.[80] In light of the recent millennial scare of the 1970's, Wilcox points out that "James Watt, Reagan's choice to head the Department of Interior, reportedly argued that the second coming of Christ meant that there was little need to preserve the environment."[81] While the Moral Majority might have maintained some level of integrity regarding their views on the central importance of the family unit within modern society, this group was very shortsighted when it came to acknowledging the inherent dignity of the marginalized: homosexuals and practitioners of other alternative lifestyles,

---

[77] Wilcox, *Onward Christian Soldiers: The Religious Right in American Politics?*, 5. The terms "New Religious Right," "New Christian Right," "New Right," etc. are often used interchangeably by various authors, and will be used as such in this research.
[78] *Ibid.*
[79] Ibid., 4-5.
[80] Ibid., 84-85.
[81] Ibid., 85. [Wilcox references the reader to Kenneth J. Wald, *Religion and Politics in the United States*. 2d edition, (Washington, DC: CQ Press, 1992).]

women, and creation itself. Concerning the Moral Majority in the state of Indiana during the early nineties, Wilcox writes, "Fully 98 percent of the Indiana Moral Majority wanted to fire public school teachers if they were discovered to be homosexual."[82]

Moving Towards 1999-The Millennial Scare Resurfaces on the American Frontier

The Religious Right controlled the political scene in the United States throughout the presidencies of Reagan and the elder George Bush, but by the early to middle nineties, their hopes and dreams for a national revival had been shattered. In 1992, liberal Democratic candidate William J. Clinton was elected as the new President of the United States, and consequently, the conservative Republicans, and more importantly, the Religious Right, lost control of the White House. Many conservative Christians began to despair that with the new millennium just on the horizon, America was on the verge of a national moral and religious crisis, and many American Christians began to prepare for and warn others about what they foresaw as God's impending judgment on the United States. Consider the words of this evangelical author regarding the election of Clinton: "Those who we have come to know as baby boomers were born between 1946 and 1964, with the first generation of baby boomers coming of age in the 1960's. Their crowning glory was the inauguration of the presidents Clinton. Their coming of age precipitated a major disintegration in the fabric of American culture."[83]

---

[82] Ibid., 120.
[83] Bob Rosio, *The Culture War in America: A Society in Chaos* (Lafayette, Louisiana: Huntington House Publishers, 1995), 30.
Notice that Rosio, rather knowingly or unknowingly, makes two key references. The reference to the baby boom generation deals with the group of youth that was born around the 1950's; just after their parents returned home from either the war, or in the case of most women, deliberate aiding in the war efforts. The return from the war symbolizes a time (the 1950's) when American society was trying to reform itself into a moral and subdued society. During the 1960's the baby boom generation subsequently reacted against the moralistic and pietistic extremes of their parents; an almost predictable pendulum swing in the opposite direction.

A Historical Overview of United States Protestant Fundamentalism

In June of 1993, Stan and Leslie Johnson of Topeka, Kansas began hosting a new fifteen minute radio program, which turned into a full-time ministry entitled "The Prophecy Club." In 1994, the first meeting of The Prophecy Club was held in Topeka, and 110 people were in attendance. The Prophecy Club began to host monthly meetings in various influential cities across the United States, and the club invited the most prominent speakers on end-time prophecy. These messages were subsequently videotaped and audiotaped, and the audiotapes were sent to Christian radio stations to be broadcasted throughout America.[84] The Prophecy Club lists the following as its main objectives:

- To make Christians more aware of the evil devices of Satan
- To warn Christians that judgment is coming to America
- To challenge God's people to stop sinning and turn to Jesus with all their heart
- To be an information source on current events in Bible prophecy[85]

As one who listened to a number of the Prophecy Club broadcasts prior to the turn of the millennium, and knew of other concerned Christians in the surrounding area who were doing the same, the author of this research can recall the fear that many of the speakers provoked in the hearts of innocent believers. Many of the doomsday prophets of The Prophecy Club testified as to what Americans could expect as a result of the Y2K

The second reference that Rosio makes to the "presidents Clinton" is most likely *not* a typographical error. Many conservative American Christians typically refer to Hillary Rodham Clinton as the true force behind the Clinton presidency, as she was an avid feminist and an outspoken supporter of various liberal causes. Rodham Clinton is presently serving in the U.S. Senate as the first former First Lady to enter into such a high level of public office; a clearly defining moment for American feminists.

[84] Editor(s) Unknown, "The Prophecy Club: About Us" Stan and Leslie Johnson, Prophecy Club Founders (Topeka Kansas: 2004) via *Internet*: <http://www.prophecyclub.com/aboutus.htm>. Accessed April, 7, 2005. The Prophecy Club identifies Ezekiel 33:6 the defining verse of its ministry: "But if the watchmen see the sword come, and blow not the trumpet, and the people be not warned; if the sword come, and take any person from among them, he is taken away in his iniquity; but his blood I will require at the watchman's hand." (Quoted from the Website- Biblical version not specified).

[85] "The Prophecy Club" via *Internet*: <http://www.prophecyclub.com/aboutus.htm>.

computer bug in the years following the turn of the millennium, and the predictions were much more dire than the average American predicted. Many reasonably concerned Americans stockpiled a few essential items, such as food and water, in case of minor complications due to the Y2K computer bug. However, certain doomsday seers within The Prophecy Club predicted a far worse case scenario for the new millennium: the declaration of martial law and a systematic rounding-up of Christians to be sent to concentration camps.[86]

If one keys in to the website of The Prophecy Club at this moment and examines the readable broadcasts that are contained among the archives, one will not find any broadcasts dated prior to 2000. However, the earliest broadcasts that this website contains are dated September/October 2000, and one of the articles is appropriately titled: "I Apologize for Taking Advantage of You Concerning Y2K."[87] In this article, Johnson asks for forgiveness to all the people who were hurt by the actions and reports of The Prophecy Club. He justifies his actions by stating:

> While I am repenting, I may as well address a few more subjects. Each month I was under tremendous pressure to make ends meet. A large part of that was determined by having an exciting new speaker…I explained it is an open platform, for their message is to be heard- a message that otherwise would not. It is like eating watermelon. Eat the meat, spit out the seeds. No one has 100% truth. We all see through a glass darkly.[88]

While Johnson claims that he has repented of his actions, it should be noted that The Prophecy Club is still in existence, and one look at the various contents of the website shows that it is continuing to utilize its previous scare tactics; while this time making reference to countless other

---

[86] The exact citations of these radio programs cannot be located, as the author heard them prior to the dawning of the millennium.

[87] Stan Johnson, "I Apologize for Taking Advantage of You Concerning Y2K," (Topeka, Kansas: September/October 2000) in "The Prophecy Club" via *Internet*: <http://www.prophecyclub.com/article_2000_sept-oct_02.htm>.

[88] Johnson, "I Apologize for Taking Advantage of You Concerning Y2K," in "The Prophecy Club" via *Internet*: <http://www.prophecyclub.com/article_2000_sept-oct_02.htm>. It is interesting to note that not too long after their Y2K predictions did not come to pass, The Prophecy Club continued selling millennial survivalist gear at a reduced price.

recent world developments. The prophetic frenzy continues, and many sincere and innocent American Christians are being scared into believing that God desires for them to live in constant fear and trepidation. In the opinion of the author, it cannot be the will of God for Christians to live in constant fear of what could happen. It is true that life is filled with its own set of struggles and tribulations, but Christians are called to live above these struggles by reflecting God's vision of justice and peace in a world that is already torn by so much chaos and self-destruction. As Christians, the last thing we are called to do is to incite fear in the lives of other believers who are joining us in the struggle of promoting the will of God on earth.

Consider this statement of the Preparatory Papers of the upcoming Commission on World Mission and Evangelism conference of the World Council of Churches to be held in Athens, Greece in May of 2005: "In a time of globalization with increasing violence, fragmentation and exclusion, the mission of the church is to receive, celebrate, proclaim and work for reconciliation, healing and fullness of life in Christ."[89] The world is already filled with troubles, and it is precisely for this reason that God has called the Christian community to take prophetic action. The Church should never add to these troubles by promoting internal spiritual turmoil.

Concluding Remarks

While United States Protestant fundamentalism is not a dangerous phenomenon within itself, its proposed method of biblical interpretation and approach to eschatological matters can have an unprecedented negative effect on the life of the sincere adherent. The fundamentalist worldview can provoke images in the mind of a believer of an unwavering vengeful deity who delights in bringing about destruction through various cataclysmic world events. However, it is through having meaningful encounters with

---

[89] Editor(s) Unknown, Commission on World Mission and Evangelism, World Council of Churches, "Theme, Thematic Area and Signposts on the Journey Towards the Athens Conference" in *WCC Conference on World Mission and Evangelism; Come Holy Spirit-Heal and Reconcile*: "Called in Christ to be Reconciling and Healing Communities, Athens, Greece, 9-16 May 2005, Preparatory Paper No. 3" (Prepared October 2003: 3:1).

more ecumenically minded Christians that such memories can be healed. Therefore, the next chapter will examine ecumenical encounters between various evangelical and non-evangelical groups in order to gain practical insights on how ecumenically minded Christians can more effectively address the spiritual concerns of their former fundamentalist neighbors, especially regarding the aforementioned topics: biblical inerrancy and eschatological matters.

Chapter Three
Evangelicals and Non-Evangelicals In Dialogue: An Overview of the Official Bilateral Dialogues in Relation to the Issues of Biblical Interpretation and Eschatology

This chapter will conduct a textual analysis of the reports of a number of official bilateral dialogues, as it will explore what these reports have to say in regards to the preselected issues of biblical interpretation and eschatology. Any relevant connections that the author finds from among the reports will be drawn as part of the overall process of analysis. Throughout this textual analysis, the author will examine how the reports of the official bilateral dialogues deal with the aforementioned theological issues, so that conclusions can be further developed as to how ecumenically minded Christians can more effectively address the spiritual and theological concerns of former fundamentalist Protestant Christians in the United States.

Evangelicals and Non-Evangelicals: Reaching A Common Understanding of Biblical Interpretation

The report, *Baptists and Reformed in Dialogue*[1] is the result of ten years worth of official bilateral consultations conducted between the World Alliance of Reformed Churches (WARC) and the Baptist World Alliance (BWA). The report itself is unclear regarding the exact dates of these dialogues, but this particular report was drafted at the final evaluation meeting in December of 1982, and the report itself states that five years of successive dialogues took place between the years of 1973 and 1977.[2] The two groups met for the following main purpose: "… to indicate more clearly the agreements and disagreements between the Baptist and Reformed traditions, and to ask how the two confessional families could grow together in deeper fellowship, in order to fulfill the common task of mission given to them by the one Lord of the Church."[3]

The Baptist World Alliance, which encompasses a wide spectrum of Baptist confessional traditions around the world, is evangelical in nature. However, it has been heavily criticized for its "liberal" orientation by the Southern Baptist Convention (SBC) within the United States, of which composed nearly half of the BWA membership in 1989.[4] The SBC officially pulled out of the BWA during the summer of 2004. The World Alliance of Reformed Churches is a similar organization that is composed of Reformed traditions from all over the world that are not known for being evangelical in nature. The Reformed tradition traces its spiritual roots back to the time of the Reformation with the theologies of Calvin and Zwingli, who joined forces with all Protestants to challenge the authority of the established church[5] and to reclaim the central authority of the scriptures and the

---

[1] WARC, *Baptists and Reformed in Dialogue* (Geneva: WARC, 1984).
[2] Ibid., 1.
[3] Ibid., 2.
[4] Ellen M. Rosenburg, *The Southern Baptists: A Subculture in Transition* (Knoxville, TN: The University of Tennesse Press, 1989), 95.
[5] For the Reformed tradition, the established church against which it was reacting was the Roman Catholic Church. For Baptists, the situation was slightly different, as they emerged from the Puritan/Congregationalist separatist movement against the perceived corruption within the Church of England [See WARC, *Baptists and Reformed in Dialogue*, 3]. It must be noted, however, that the Baptist tradition was formed more around the

right of the individual Christian to read and interpret the scriptures for oneself, echoing the Reformation cry for "sola scriptura, " which is Latin for "scripture alone."[6]

In the attempts of the BWA and WARC to establish some common ground, the report states, "'It is interesting to observe that historically the theology of Calvin and Zwingli has had a very great influence on the development of Baptist thinking since the Reformation,'"[7] even though traditionally, Baptists trace their spiritual roots back to "…the first baptisms of believers carried out by John Smyth among the English exiles in Amsterdam in the years 1608-09.[8] Likewise, the report points out that the Calvinist Baptists, another group of Baptists from England, adopted the Westminster Confession, thereby serving as an historic link between the Baptist and Reformed (Scottish Presbyterian) traditions.[9] Although this point is not mentioned in the BWA/WARC document, it is also important to note that whenever one considers the history of evangelicalism in the United States regarding the doctrine of biblical inerrancy, the Princeton theology of Hodge and Warfield, who both belonged to the Calvinist (Reformed) tradition, further serves as a contextual link between the Baptists and Reformed groups within the United States.

After establishing a common historical basis from which to begin their discussions, the Baptist and Reformed groups establish a common

---

central concern of adult baptism, as many were labeled "Anabaptists" or re-baptisers, while most churches within the Reformed tradition (one exception is the Christian Church (Disciples of Christ)), practice infant baptism, acknowledging the grace that accompanies the child throughout life, and then requiring a moment of confirmation of faith at an age when the child can decide for oneself whether or not to follow the faith into which one has been baptized and nurtured.

[6] "Sola Fide," (faith alone), "solus Christus," (Christ alone), "sola scriptura," (scripture alone), and sola gratia (grace alone) were also other predominant concerns of the Reformation era, [See General Conference of Seventh-Day Adventists and the Lutheran World Federation, "Report of the Bilateral Conversations" (Cartigny/Switzerland, 15 May 1998) in *Lutherans and Adventists in Conversation* (Silver Springs, Maryland, USA: General Conference of Seventh-day Adventists and Geneva, Switzerland: Lutheran World Federation, 2000), 5-23: 8.] but for the purpose of this research, the central focus will be placed on the doctrine of "sola scriptura."

[7] WARC, *Baptists and Reformed in Dialogue*, 8.

[8] Ibid., 3.

[9] *Ibid.*

doctrinal basis: "'It can also be noted that both traditions share a common emphasis on the normative source of Holy Scripture, the central place of the Word of God, the witness to Jesus Christ as Saviour and Lord, the sovereignty of grace.'"[10] Both groups also acknowledge a common objective as believers in the message of Jesus the Christ, "Further, both traditions have a common concern to live out today a witness and service in the obedience of faith."[11] As one can see in the example of this dialogue that one viable way to begin challenging preconceived notions of the "other" is to pinpoint the commonalities shared by both sides: in terms of history and belief.

Such an approach was also taken in the official report of the 1994-1998 Lutheran/Adventist bilateral consultations, entitled *Lutherans and Adventists in Conversation*, which records the results of a series of bilateral dialogues conducted between the Lutheran World Federation (LWF) and the General Conference of Seventh-day Adventists.[12] Although the Adventist movement clearly traces its beginnings back to nineteenth century America, the report from Darmstadt of November 1-5, 1994 concluded, "It quickly became clear that the strong appreciation among the SDA theologians for the work of Martin Luther formed a natural starting point for the interchange."[13] Just as the Baptists and Reformed traditions trace their common spiritual heritage back to the European Reformation, Lutherans and Adventists, and for that matter, the majority of other United States Protestant groups can do the same.

While individual reasons for splitting from the established churches during the Reformation differed from group to group, one central concern of all the groups was essentially the same: freedom of biblical interpretation, which is centered around the Reformation doctrine of "sola scriptura."[14] Even the doctrinal issues, which originally seemed so divisive among the denominations that came out of the Reformation, such as the Anabaptist concern for the correct nature and proper administration of baptism, or the Lutheran debate between faith and works, were based on disagreements

---

[10] Ibid., 8.
[11] *Ibid.*
[12] SDA and LWF, *Lutherans and Adventists in Conversation (Silver Springs, Maryland/ Geneva, Switzerland: GCSDA and LWF, 2000).*
[13] Ibid., 6.
[14] Ibid., 12.

concerning a proper understanding of the nature of biblical interpretation.[15] All evangelical and non-evangelical U.S. Protestant groups alike, including the fundamentalist groups, can trace their common spiritual heritages back to one central issue: the nature and goal of biblical interpretation, therefore affirming their common concern for the preservation of an unshattered confidence in the centrality of the scriptures.

The Baptist/Reformed dialogue states, "Both the Reformed and the Baptist traditions share a common emphasis on Holy Scripture as the normative source for faith and practice."[16] Furthermore, both sides admit that there is much more to biblical interpretation than a mere reading of what is written on the page and interpreting it in light of what it seems to say.[17] Such a surface reading of any sacred literature deprives it of its richness, and to a large extent, its sacredness. However, this approach creates a major dilemma among many Protestant denominations, each of which acknowledges that it was founded upon the right of the individual believer to read and interpret the biblical texts for oneself.

In order to further complicate matters, the more conservative denominations claim that the scriptures are inspired by the Holy Spirit. Therefore, whenever a Christian, who has the Holy Spirit indwelling within, reads and interprets the inspired scriptures, such an interpretation can never be wrong, because the Holy Spirit, who cannot lie, illuminates the mind of the believer.[18] However, when confronted with this dilemma, the more liberal-minded Christian will most likely respond, "Is not everyone ready to find his [*sic*] own opinion in the Scripture?"[19] Furthermore, while both Lutherans and Adventists join their Baptist and Reformed siblings in affirming the centrality of the scriptures, each group claims certain guiding theological criterion on which all biblical interpretation subsequently rests:

---

[15] Luther himself had a compelling insight on the dilemma between faith and works as he was searching the scriptures one day. This was the event that prompted Luther to make known his desire for reform within the Roman Catholic Church.
[16] WARC, *Baptists and Reformed in Dialogue*, 11.
[17] *Ibid.*
[18] Of course, this does not eliminate the questions of sin or the sheer limitations of humanity.
[19] WARC, *Baptists and Reformed in Dialogue*, 12.

For Lutherans, the gospel understood as unmerited justification, is the organic center of Scripture; it is the hermeneutical key to the study and interpretation of Scripture. Adventists look to the totality of Scripture, seeking to find Christ as the center and the New Testament as the summit of Scripture. Further, in their study, Adventists tend to seek explicit biblical proofs, whereas Lutherans leave more room for what is not explicitly stated (e.g. Sunday observance). Thus, Adventists, while alert to the historical background of the biblical writings, apply Scripture more directly to life today. Lutherans tend to relate specific passages to the total message of Scripture and also give particular attention to the changed conditions of today's world.[20]

One way to remedy this concern is to point out that every confessional tradition reads the scriptures through its own hermeneutical lenses.[21] As the WARC report points out, "…every theological opinion has not only 'theological grounds', but also different (psychological, sociological, cultural, etc.) 'causes', of which we have to be (and are more and more) aware."[22] In other words, one cannot separate the reader from the culture in which she or he resides. As the above quotation indirectly suggests, both Lutherans and Adventists read the scriptures in accordance with modern times: Adventists search the scriptures for explicit answers to the struggles of daily life, while Lutherans try to interpret what they see as the overall biblical message in light of the changing conditions in modern society.[23]

No text, whether religious or secular, can ever truly speak for itself; there is always a reader present to interpret it in light of his or her subjective experiences. This is an important point that an ecumenically minded Christian can point out to a former fundamentalist who is struggling with the question, "Will I, in leaving fundamentalism, lose the support of biblical authority?"[24] For the ecumenically minded Christian, it is important to realize that both conservative and liberal Protestants (and all other Christians) share one undeniable characteristic in common: an

---

[20] SDA and LWF, *Lutherans and Adventists in Conversation*, 13.
[21] WARC, *Baptists and Reformed in Dialogue*, 11.
[22] Ibid., 11-12.
[23] SDA and LWF, *Lutherans and Adventists in Conversation*, 13.
[24] Barr, *Escaping from Fundamentalism*, ix.

Evangelicals and Non-Evangelicals in Dialogue

experiential approach to the scriptures. For the former fundamentalist, the knowledge that all denominations share this common characteristic can prove to be a liberating insight.

Interestingly, the American Pentecostal Movement, an evangelical movement which includes churches from the North, as well as from the Central and South Americas, met with the Office of Church and Ecumenical Relations of the WCC in San Jose, Costa Rica in 1996, approaches the scriptures in the following way, as indicated in a report entitled *Consultation With Pentecostals in the Americas*:[25] "For Pentecostals, the Bible is a story and they read that story into their lives and their lives into that story."[26] This hermeneutical approach is based on the belief that the Holy Spirit, who indwells both the scriptures and the life of the believer, deciphers the meaning of the words of the ancient text as they apply to the life of the believer in her or his immediate context.[27] In other words, the Holy Spirit gleans eternal truths from the text as they apply to the concrete historical situation. Once again, this approach can be compared to that of the Lutherans, who "…relate specific passages to the total message of Scripture and also give particular attention to the changed conditions of today's world.[28] In both instances, one is dealing with the ongoing task of applying the solutions offered by the biblical texts to needs of the present world. On some level, every modern Christian is engaged in this common hermeneutical task.

Once the former fundamentalist is made aware of the high level of continuity that exists between the contextual situation of the former denomination and its overriding approach to the scriptures, he or she

---

[25] Huibert van Beek, ed. *Consultation With Pentecostals in the Americas: San Jose, Costa Rica 4-8 June 1996*. Office of Church and Ecumenical Relations, World Council of Churches (World Council of Churches: Geneva, n.d.).

[26] Richard D. Israel, "Pentecostal Spirituality and the Use of Scripture" in *Consultations With Pentecostals in the Americas*, ed. van Beek, 45-55: 50.

[27] Israel, "Pentecostal Spirituality and the Use of Scripture" in *Consultations With Pentecostals in the Americas*, 51. Israel writes, "The Paraclete, abiding and indwelling Spirit of Truth, guides into truth and teaches all things (John 14-17). This indwelling of the believer by the Spirit assures the Spirit's presence to teach believers as they read the Spirit's inscripturated words." It is also interesting to note that Pentecostals do not see the personal message given by the Holy Spirit as "…necessarily tied to the grammatical sense of the biblical text." (p. 51).

[28] SDA and LWF, *Lutherans and Adventists in Conversation*, 13.

will begin to see its interpretive methods as culturally conditioned, and therefore, limited. This insight will prove to be liberating in terms of the way that the recovering fundamentalist approaches the biblical texts, and consequently, God. God will no longer appear as the authoritarian defender of the inerrant scriptures who delights in revealing unchanging, eternal truths to one group of "chosen" people as they read the biblical texts, but as the defender of all people who uses the diverse authors of the scriptures to speak eternal truths about the human condition in light of unique historical situations. Such a realization will encourage former fundamentalists to seek out the insights of other Christians- not only in the United States (or their respective countries of origin), but all over the world- regarding other possible methods of biblical interpretation, and these encounters will lead to newfound freedom in the life of the former fundamentalist in terms of improving his or her relationship with God and others. Such ecumenical encounters may even lead the former fundamentalist to consider previously unconsidered or forbidden options in terms of major life decisions and ministerial callings.

Methods of Biblical Interpretation and Their Influence on Eschatological Approaches:

A Focus on the Seventh-day Adventists and the Lutherans

The way that any one religious group interprets the biblical texts undoubtedly has a strong impact on the way that any group interprets eschatological references within the scriptures. Given the historic apocalyptic orientation of the Adventists, the Lutherans and Adventists devote a great amount of time and energy to this issue. Both groups begin by affirming that their common approach to eschatological issues is based on their common understandings of Jesus.[29] This understanding is based on the way that they both view Jesus as presented within the scriptures:

> Both Lutherans and Adventists affirm that Jesus Christ is the center of eschatology. He is the Lord of time and space, and his atoning death on

---

[29] SDA and LWF, *Lutherans and Adventists in Conversation*, 18.

the cross has won the decisive battle over the forces of evil and ensured the ultimate restoration of all things. 'For God was pleased to have all his [sic] fulness dwell in him, and through him to reconcile to himself all things, whether things in earth, or things in heaven, by making peace through his blood, shed on the cross' (Col. 1:19, 20).[30]

Both groups share a Christocentric view of the scriptures. They see Jesus as the center and goal of both the Hebrew Scriptures and the New Testament. Both groups also believe that this understanding of scripture is only possible because of the atoning death of Jesus on the cross, which caused a complete breakthrough in the way that humankind and creation relates to God. The report states, "Lutherans and Adventists affirm that history is not cyclical but linear, not random but moving toward its telos (goal) in a cosmic restoration."[31] Due to the atoning death of Jesus on the cross, all creation will someday be reconciled to God.

However, in spite of their agreement on the aforementioned issues, the two groups do not share similar views on "…the respective understandings and exposition of biblical apocalyptic literature."[32] While Lutherans have traditionally been hesitant to apply apocalyptic texts to modern times, focusing more on the historical nature of book of Revelation, as it applies to the situation of the early Church, Adventists believe that the apocalyptic sayings of scripture are meant for a specific purpose: to promote awareness among believers of the flow of history as it moves towards the eschaton.[33] For the Adventist, apocalyptic literature "…is not for the purpose of satisfying idle curiosity, but to confirm faith in Christ as Lord of history."[34]

Whenever Adventists interpret apocalyptic literature in light of present day events, they do not focus on specific apocalyptic symbols as representing key world figures or specific events, but they focus more on how the symbols relate to the broader scope of recent historical developments. The Adventist participants in this dialogue realize that mistakes have been made

---

[30] SDA and LWF, *Lutherans and Adventists in Conversation*, 18.
[31] *Ibid.*
[32] Ibid., 19.
[33] Ibid., 20.
[34] *Ibid.*

in the past regarding Adventist apocalyptic predictions; nevertheless they are careful to maintain their position that the biblical texts can still provide important clues regarding the apocalyptic scope of history. However, like the Lutherans, they do not ignore the historical background of the texts.[35] Regarding such issues, the report states:

> Adventists hold that the symbols, numbers and beasts of Daniel and the Apocalypse give- in the broad sense, not in detail- the course of human history. This they do by letting Scripture interpret itself and considering the historical setting of each document. At times, some Adventists have erred in claiming to understand details rather than the broad sweep, and have made misguided statements about the future which only God can know. Adventists seek to avoid such excesses; nevertheless, they are convinced that their historicist approach to interpretation remains valid.[36]

Many people have regarded Luther as an apocalypticist, as he interpreted the events of his world in light of certain apocalyptic scriptures. He believed, along with many Christians at the beginning of the 16th century, that he lived in the last days, and that the Pope was the Antichrist.[37] Luther could even be seen as an apocalyptic date-setter in regards to the millennial reign of Christ: "In his 1530 Preface to the Book of Revelation he wrote: '…the thousand years are to begin about the time this book was written, and…the devil was bound-although the reckoning need not be exactly to the minute. After the Turks, the Last Judgment follows quickly.'"[38]

Just as Adventists trace their beginnings back to the apocalyptic predictions of Miller and White, Lutherans cannot erase such predictions

---

[35] *Ibid.*
[36] *Ibid.*
[37] Jorg Rothermundt, "Eschatology in the Lutheran Perspective" in *Lutherans and Adventists in Conversation*, 276-290: 279-280.
[38] Erwin Buck, "How Lutherans Read the Bible" in *Lutherans and Adventists in Conversation*, 58-71: 69. [Buck quotes from Luther, "Preface to Revelation" (1522), vol. 35, p. 409.] In regards to the Turks, Luther is most likely referring the invasion of the Ottoman empire around this time, seeing this as a holy war that will bring about the inauguration of the millennial reign of the Christ.

from their denominational history, although modern Lutherans do not take this approach to eschatological issues. Luther's apocalyptic leanings eventually gave way to his even heavier emphasis on the daily presence of salvation in the life of the believer.[39] For modern Lutherans, as well as for many modern Adventist groups, eschatology encompasses more than just the distant future. It is an ever-present reality in the immediate context of daily life. According to the official report, both groups affirm:

> For the believer in Jesus, eschatology has both a present and a future dimension. The person who is justified by grace alone through faith alone has already passed from death to life (Col. 3:3) and already sits with Christ in the heavenly places (Eph. 2:6), and a child of God (1 John 3:1,2), no longer living in terror or uncertainty before God.[40]

Whether or not a religious group interprets apocalyptic texts in light of recent or foreseen historical developments always remains an irresolvable dilemma in ecumenical relations. Whenever a certain group makes specific eschatological predictions or interprets apocalyptic passages in a particular way, there are often presumptions on the part of the proponents of these positions that those who do not share the same worldview will be caught unaware when the judgments of the eschaton fall upon the world. This understanding paints a picture of God as the exclusive, authoritarian guardian of all truth, who only chooses to communicate information regarding the events of the eschaton to a select few. Due to this understanding, these groups develop elitist attitudes towards others who do not share the same worldview. They view the "other" as spiritually deficient, and therefore, unworthy to have received certain revealed truths regarding the actual state of world affairs.

However, the final part of the above quotation provides a critical suggestion as to how Christians of varying eschatological opinions can more effectively recognize the legitimacy of other faith claims. If any two Christian groups disagree with one another concerning the proper order of

---

[39] Rothermundt, "Eschatology in the Lutheran Perspective" in *Lutherans and Adventists in Conversation*, 280.
[40] SDA and LWF, "Report of the Bilateral Conversations" in *Lutherans and Adventists in Conversation*, 18.

eschatological events, both groups should find consolation in the fact that if they affirm together that "...Jesus Christ is the center of eschatology...the Lord of time and space...",[41] neither group should have to worry about the possibility of the other group "...living in terror or uncertainty before God."[42] In spite of the fact the two groups might not share the same apocalyptic worldview, the fact that the non-eschatologically oriented group also affirms a belief in Jesus as the author and timeless guardian of all world events, should serve as consolation to their apocalyptically concerned counterparts that they (the former group) will not be led astray in the end. Even the visions of Ellen G. White testified to the fact that only the people who took their eyes off Jesus fell into darkness.[43] In the end, having the correct doctrine regarding the eschaton was secondary to the centrality of Jesus, around whom all such doctrines are built.

Whenever ecumenically minded Christians are addressing the concerns of former fundamentalists who have been victimized by extreme forms of apocalypticism, they can console their former fundamentalist sisters and brothers with the following insights, which are made evident throughout the above analysis of the official report of the Lutheran/Adventist bilateral dialogues. The first insight is that most denominations can locate certain moments in their histories when apocalyptic matters were high on their lists of spiritual and theological concerns, and many such religious groups can even identify key apocalyptic enthusiasts within their respective traditions who made erroneous predictions concerning the order of events on the eschatological timetable. A former fundamentalist might even be surprised to discover that Luther himself made faulty predictions concerning the end of time. Such knowledge can be comforting to a recovering fundamentalist, who is dealing with the guilt of having fallen into the trap of believing such unsound dogmatic claims.

The second insight that this report offers is that whatever approach any given denomination takes regarding eschatological issues, the central object around which all eschatological concerns (among most Christian

---

[41] SDA and LWF, "Report of the Bilateral Conversations" in *Lutherans and Adventists in Conversation*, 18.
[42] *Ibid*.
[43] White, "My First Vision" in "Early Writings," 13-31: 15, via *Internet*: <http://english.sdaglobal.org/dnl/books/images/ew.htm#20>.

denominations) are centered remains the same: Jesus, who is proclaimed by the Church as the Christ. For the former fundamentalist, who is dealing with traumas caused by exposure to images of end-time events as portrayed in rapture movies and by groups such as The Prophecy Club, the realization that the events of the eschaton are secondary to the message of God's unconditional love, as it is found in Jesus the Christ, can prove to be healing. To the recovering fundamentalist, a shift of emphasis from the impending wrath of the apocalypse, to the all-encompassing love of the one in whom the events of the apocalypse rest, proves to be an effective remedy for all such fears. If Christians take the belief seriously that the character of God was revealed in the life of Jesus of Nazareth, they can also find comfort in the realization that God is not a malicious tyrant who delights in imposing endless condemnation on the world, but instead, is willing to make self-sacrifices for the sake of the world.

The Baptist/Reformed Contribution

While the report from the Baptist/Reformed dialogue does not specifically address the issue of eschatology, it stresses the centrality of Jesus as the initiator and bearer of the covenant between God and humankind: "We agree in seeing the 'newness' of the new covenant in Jesus Christ himself, in the eschatological significance of his person and work in the eschatological gift of the Spirit (cf. Heb. 3:10, I Cor. 11:23-25)."[44] The report continues to affirm, "The one church belongs to the one Lord. It is built, assembled and sustained by him…for the Word which sustains it became flesh (John 1:14)."[45] If Jesus the Christ remains the one solid foundation of the Church, this should leave a lot of room for differences of opinion regarding trivial issues, such as methods of scriptural interpretation and the order of eschatological events.

The Church, as the representative of Christ on earth, has so much more with which to concern itself, because it exists for one main purpose: to point the way to an abundant life in Christ. If Christians of differing confessional traditions continue to condemn one another over

---

[44] WARC, *Baptists and Reformed in Dialogue*, 13.
[45] Ibid., 27.

disagreements concerning the correct interpretation of key apocalyptic texts, the world will think that the central message of Jesus is one of hatred and impending judgment. Such an uncaring and inharmonious Church provides the world with a distorted picture of the very person it is called to represent- Jesus of Nazareth- who is affirmed by Christians to be the embodiment of God's unconditional love and acceptance to the religious and political outcasts of his society.

The Seventh-Day Adventists and the World Council of Churches: Working Towards a Responsible Eschatology

Reaching agreement on the correct interpretation of apocalyptic texts is never an easy task for Christians of any tradition. In the late 1960's, the World Council of Churches held official consultations with the Seventh-day Adventists on different topics, one of which included eschatology. Along with eschatological concerns, a heavy emphasis was also placed on the importance of biblical interpretation, especially in regards to apocalyptic texts. Throughout their discussions, both groups came to a consensus that they could learn from one another in regards to how to approach these texts. It was acknowledged by both sides that it is the task of all churches "…to interpret the signs."[46] However, the exact nature of these "signs," or the correct way to interpret them remains unclear: "Can this interpretation be derived directly from the Bible or must it be discerned under the guidance of the Spirit in each situation? Who interprets the signs? The individual, the Church as a whole? Which are the signs?"[47] So many crucial questions remain unanswered.

It is clear to many Christians that the present world situation is in serious trouble, spiritually, as well as politically, environmentally, economically, and on so many other levels. As the earthly representative of Christ on earth, the Church needs to adopt a responsible eschatology

---

[46] Lukas Vischer, Director of the Secretariat of the Commission on Faith and Order, "Analysis of Discussion on 'Apocalyptic Prophecy'" in *The World Council of Churches/Seventh-Day Adventist Conversations and their Significance*, Faith and Order Paper No. 55, Reprinted from *The Ecumenical Review* Vol. XXII No. 2-April 1970 (Switzerland: World Council of Churches, n.d.), 7-9: 9.
[47] *Ibid.*

that takes all of these concerns into careful consideration. Therefore, ecumenically minded Christians need to take more seriously the concerns of their fellow fundamentalist and evangelical sisters and brothers when it comes to discerning the "signs of the times." The report is clear in addressing this concern: "Do non-Adventist Christians not often remain too vague in their witness, not having the courage to interpret the signs of the times?"[48] At the same time, more conservatively minded Christians need to pay more attention to the *discernment* aspect of "discerning" the "signs of the times." The report equally asks of Adventists: "Do they not too quickly establish a link between certain texts and certain events?"[49]

Both extremes can be equally dangerous. If Christians ignore the eschatological dimension of their faith, they will be caught unaware whenever certain events take the world by surprise. At the same time, an exclusivist focus on the events of the eschaton can be dangerous, producing elitist and escapist attitudes on the part of the believer. There is a need to develop a healthy approach to eschatological matters. While such an approach needs to take current events into consideration, it must never neglect the eternal perspective of history.[50] The report states:

> Attention should not be detracted from events which seem to determine our immediate future (e.g. secularization, the growing together of mankind [*sic*], racial problems, etc.; in comparison to these the papacy seems to be a factor of minor importance which less obscures the meaning of the Gospel). On the other hand, the Seventh-day Adventist participants felt that the WCC emphasis on current events, which seem to determine mankind's present and near future, tends to neglect the vertical dimension.[51]

While it is difficult to pinpoint the elements of a balanced eschatology, it is clear that such prophetic texts contain an undeniable ethical dimension that is often ignored by apocalypticists. While the report poses the concern

---

[48] Vischer, "Analysis of Discussion on 'Apocalyptic Prophecy'" in *The World Council of Churches/Seventh Adventist Conversations and their Significance*, 9
[49] *Ibid.*
[50] *Ibid.*
[51] *Ibid.* The reference to the papacy within this quotation is in conjunction with the common SDA concern with identifying the Pope as Antichrist.

the WCC placing too much emphasis on "…the ethical and paranetical elements in the prophetic and apocalyptic texts…"[52] the question could just as easily be turned around to ask why the SDA does not place equal emphasis on the ethical demands of the prophetic and apocalyptic texts. Whenever the Hebrew prophets or the apocalypticists of the New Testament make apocalyptic predictions, they do so for a reason. In most situations, the community-in-question neglects the ethical dimension of life. The governments that are usually criticized by the Hebrew prophets commit horrendous actions, such as using the religious establishment for the purpose of cheating people and exploiting orphans and widows. By the time of the New Testament, the ethical state of the world has not changed, except governments are now operating in close connection with the religious establishment for the mass persecution of Christians. Today, the world stage remains the same with different actors. The prophetic and apocalyptic texts may indeed still have something important to say to the current world situation.

Christians cannot afford to ignore these "signs of the times." The world is truly facing perilous days, as people are becoming more and more materialistic in the name of religion at the expense of innocent people and the earth. Christians have a responsibility to name the injustices that are perpetrated against humanity and the environment and to work towards promoting peace and justice in the world. At the same time, Christians cannot neglect the "vertical dimension"[53] of their faith. They must make it known that this world is a gift from God, and that all human beings have a mutual responsibility to care for one another and for creation, regardless of culture or creed.

Whenever ecumenically minded Christians are ministering to the concerns of their former fundamentalist brothers and sisters who testify to having been manipulated by apocalyptic extremist groups, and at the same time, are afraid to reject certain aspects of apocalyptic thought, the aforementioned conclusions can help former fundamentalists to see that it is possible to adopt a balanced approach to eschatological matters. Recovering fundamentalists will find this approach comforting, because it

---

[52] *Ibid.*
[53] Vischer, "Analysis of Discussion on 'Apocalyptic Prophecy'" in *The World Council of Churches/Seventh-Day Adventist Conversations and their Significance*, 9.

does not promote a constant source of fear in the life of the believer, and at the same time, they will find it responsible, because it calls for prophetic action- decrying the evils of unjust power structures in the world and working to promote the inherent dignity of all people and creation. Such an approach will be reassuring in that it will not only allow for creativity in biblical interpretation, but it will invite the former fundamentalist to contribute to making the ideals of the Reign of God a reality on earth. Such a responsible approach to eschatology invites one to fully realize the actuality of the Reign of God in one's daily life, as opposed to living in morbid fear of it, and consequently, God.

Chapter Four
Conclusion and Implications for Ministry and Ecumenical Relations

A Brief Review of the Project Thus Far

The purpose of this thesis is to conduct a textual analysis of certain official bilateral dialogues conducted between evangelicals and non-evangelicals to determine if any ideas can be taken from among these reports which will answer the question of how ecumenically minded Christians could more effectively address the spiritual and theological concerns of former fundamentalists in the United States, and in doing so, help promote healing and reconciliation in their lives. In this textual analysis, the author will examine and establish connections among the various documents regarding how they deal with the issues of biblical interpretation and eschatology. Since evangelical Christians closely resemble fundamentalist Christians in belief and practice, the objective of this textual analysis is to provide an answer to the question of how these reports can be further employed in order to promote understanding and sensitivity among ecumenically minded Christians regarding the past experiences of former fundamentalists.

This project begins by defining terms, such as "fundamentalist," "ecumenically minded Christian," and "spiritual and theological concerns."

Conclusion and Implications for Ministry and Ecumenical Relations

Next, this thesis addresses the assumptions of the author and the reasons for conducting this research project. It continues by establishing a brief historical context for Protestant fundamentalism in the United States and includes a review of literature addressing this topic. Finally, it addresses the objectives and methodology of this research and the scope and limitations of this project.

The second chapter presents a more extensive overview of the historical context and worldview of United States fundamentalism as this phenomenon is found in a nation where separation between church and state is both a political and religious reality. This cultural situation lends itself to a variety of religious expressions that eventually crystallize into distinct creeds and practices that become normative expressions of the Christian faith for all who unite with that religious community. The difficulty in removing oneself from this sphere of influence often creates problems for those who are searching for a spiritual home outside the fundamentalist community. It is the belief and observation of the author that the more ecumenically minded Christians, who receive their former fundamentalist sisters and brothers into their churches, do not know how to properly respond to the spiritual and theological concerns of the former fundamentalists who seek refuge in the care of their ecclesial fellowship.

Chapter three conducts a textual analysis of certain bilateral dialogues held between evangelicals and non-evangelicals in order to determine what these reports have to contribute to helping ecumenically minded Christians more effectively address the spiritual and theological concerns of former fundamentalists, especially in regards to the issues of biblical interpretation and eschatology. The first chapter suggested that this thesis would refer to dialogues among Lutherans and Adventists, as recorded in *Lutherans and Adventists in Conversation: Report and Papers Presented 1994-1998*, and the dialogues among the Baptist and Reformed traditions, as recorded in *Baptists and Reformed in Dialogue: Documents from the Conversations Sponsored by the World Alliance of Reformed Churches and the Baptist World Alliance*, both of which proved helpful in the research.

The first chapter had also listed a number of reports to which reference would be made as needed. Although all reports were consulted, chapter three only made reference to two reports among the entire list, both of which were conducted by the WCC and a specified evangelical group: *Consultation with Pentecostals in the Americas*, to which a brief reference was made in regards to the issue of biblical interpretation, and *The World Council of Churches/Seventh-Day Adventist Conversations and their Significance*, which is a seemingly outdated report from the early seventies that devoted much attention to the issue of eschatology. It was actually this latter text that unexpectedly provided the most valuable insights as to how ecumenically minded and former fundamentalist Christians can address the issue of eschatology together in a responsible manner that promotes healing in the life of the former fundamentalist, and at the same time, challenges other Christian groups to revaluate their approaches to eschatology.

Due to a textual analysis of the reports of the aforementioned bilateral dialogues dealing with the preselected issues of biblical interpretation and eschatology, the following conclusions were reached: (1) every confessional tradition shares an experiential approach to the scriptures, which means that life experience will always influence the way that one views the scriptures[1] (2) most denominations can pinpoint moments within their histories when apocalyptic matters were high on their lists of spiritual concerns, and many such religious groups, whether or not they are fundamentalist, can identify key apocalyptic enthusiasts who made predictions concerning various apocalyptic events, (3) for most Christians, Jesus of Nazareth, who is called the Christ, remains the center of all eschatological concerns, and finally, (4) Christians cannot afford to ignore the "signs of the times." At the same time, they cannot ignore the ethical dimension of the apocalyptic and prophetic texts. Christians need to develop a responsible and balanced approach to eschatology. Liberal and conservative Christian groups can learn from one another concerning the proper way to deal with these complex issues.

This study provided an affirmative answer to the central concern of this thesis: that the conclusions that emerged from the reports of bilateral dialogues held between evangelicals and non-evangelicals can be applied to provide vital insights regarding how ecumenically minded Christians can more effectively address the spiritual and theological concerns of former fundamentalist Christians. However, it must be stated that the

---

[1] It must be noted that even if one tries to interpret the biblical texts through the lenses of historical critical analysis, or other interpretive methods, such methods are historically conditioned, as they are influenced by a certain contextual assumptions and biases.

conclusions reached in this thesis, up until this point, could just as easily be applied to a situation involving ecumenically minded Christians and former Protestant fundamentalists outside of the United States, as well as within the North American context. The phenomenon of Protestant fundamentalism is global. However, given the unique historical situation of the United States, it is the assumption of the author that the influence of most U.S. fundamentalist denominations has the likelihood to be more pronounced.

The question that must now be addressed is where an ecumenically minded Christian from the United States can go from here in implementing these results into a ministry for former American Protestant fundamentalist Christians. The former fundamentalist will undoubtedly look to the more open-minded Christian for counseling in these spiritual and theological matters. Therefore, the more ecumenically minded Christian needs to be ready to offer her or his insights on such matters, so that healing and reconciliation can occur in the life of the recovering fundamentalist.

The Next Step: Ministering to the Spiritual and Theological Concerns of Former Fundamentalists in the United States

Part I: Dealing With Issues of Biblical Interpretation

All Christians, regardless of their respective denominations, share an experiential approach to the scriptures. This means that context always has an influence on how one interprets the biblical texts. Even if one believes that one has an objective approach to the scriptures, that approach is culturally conditioned. Therefore, if each church clings to its own understanding of the scriptures and does not look beyond the confines of its own tradition for further assistance in this task, the religious life of that church has the potential to become stagnant. However, whenever one opens the doors for new possibilities of biblical interpretation, such as the historical critical method or a liberation reading, the results can be both surprising and humbling.

For one who is emerging from Protestant fundamentalism, such a powerful realization that every act of biblical interpretation is influenced by one's context can open doors to countless previously unconsidered possibilities for facing the future. Especially within the North American context, such a realization can prove to be eye opening. Although the world is filled with almost unlimited traces of American culture, due to the phenomenon of globalization, many Americans, especially in the remote rural areas, remain sheltered within their own communities. Therefore, they are largely oblivious to the world around them. It is only when an individual becomes educated concerning the wider context of existence that their eyes are truly open to the harsh realities of the world. They begin to see that not everyone is born into the same experience, and therefore, everyone will see the world from a different perspective due to her or his unique experiences.

Life circumstances have an undeniable bearing on biblical interpretation. For instance, if one is suffering under political oppression, one will most likely view the biblical texts through the lenses of a liberation perspective. Likewise, if one is undergoing either political or religious persecution, or fears going through such persecution in the future, one can just as easily take comfort in apocalyptic literature and view the scriptures from an eschatological perspective. Experiences influence how one sees the world and how one interprets the movement of the hand of God in the world. Consider this statement:

> Read against the background of martyrdom and exile, it is not surprising that so many Christians look for promises that their sufferings are only temporary, and that God will intervene directly to save the situation. In this context, the book of Revelation looks like true prophecy on an epic scale, however unpopular or discredited it may be for most Americans or Europeans. In the South, Revelation simply makes sense, in its description of a world ruled by monstrous demonic powers. These forces might be literal servants of Satan, or symbols of evil social forces, but in either case, they are indisputably real.[2]

Whenever an ecumenically minded Christian is discussing the issue of biblical interpretation with a former Protestant fundamentalist Christian from the United States, one suggestion that could help widen the perspective

---

[2] Philip Jenkins, *The Next Christendom: The Coming of Global Christianity* (New York: Oxford University Press, 2002), 219.

Conclusion and Implications for Ministry and Ecumenical Relations

of the former fundamentalist regarding the issue of biblical interpretation is to introduce him or her to theological literature from non-western parts of the world.[3] In this case, the range of possible literature from which to consult is limitless. The ecumenical Christian can then proceed to encourage the former fundamentalist to critically assess the cultural and historical situations of that group and to draw parallels between that group's methods of scriptural interpretation and its unique cultural situation. This will help the former fundamentalist to see more clearly the impact of the contextual climate on the practice of biblical interpretation.

Finally, in examining different expressions of Christianity from all over the world, the ecumenical Christian can encourage the former fundamentalist to ask pertinent questions concerning the contextual situations that give rise to such a theology. This will lead the reader to ask more questions regarding the ethical implications surrounding such an interpretation: if the theological approach is reacting against an oppressive system, if it is being used to suppress a certain group of people, if this method of interpretation is feeding the deep-seated fears of a particular group of

---

[3] In *Escaping From Fundamentalism,* James Barr suggests that the former fundamentalist explore readings from the Catholic (Roman Catholic, as well as Orthodox and Anglican traditions) and liberal Protestant traditions He continues by briefly addressing the general level of mistrust that many Protestant fundamentalists hold towards Roman Catholicism (see 165). It should be added that within the United States, such anti-Catholic sentiments among fundamentalist Christians, as well as a general fear of feminist and liberation theologies, are perhaps more pronounced, as they are considered to promote "left wing" or "communist" ideals that go against the American radical individualist, free-market mindset. (One historic example is the election of President Kennedy, a devout Roman Catholic, as many Americans were afraid that all of Kennedy's political decisions would have to be approved by the Vatican.) Therefore, whenever an ecumenically minded Christian introduces such readings to former fundamentalists, one should always proceed with caution, as the former fundamentalist might still hold some of these anti-Catholic or anti-liberal sentiments. In this case, the best suggestion that can be offered is to encourage the reader to consider the writings purely from the perspective of scriptural interpretation, minus the popular theological labels. Encourage the person to observe how the "other" approaches the scriptures, in order to see God's hand in the midst of their specific cultural situations. Such an inquiry will show the former fundamentalist that there countless other possibilities for approaching the same text. One does not have to advocate one approach over another, but to encourage the reader to be open to the leading of the Holy Spirit in considering such methods of interpretation. If the reader keeps an open mind, he or she could be pleasantly surprised.

people, or if it is challenging the people to transcend themselves in ways that promote God's vision of justice in the world. This critical approach will help the reader to see that there are both healthy and unhealthy ways to interpret the biblical texts. The same text can simultaneously be used to promote justice or oppression- life or death.

A Sample Bible Study

One example of a biblical passage that has so often been misused for the purpose of justifying oppression within the Southeastern United States is Genesis 9: 20-27, which is the passage in which Noah curses Canaan, the son of Ham, because Ham "…saw the nakedness of his father, and told his two brothers outside" (Genesis 9:22 RSV). In this passage, Noah curses Canaan and declares that he will become the slave of his fathers' brothers (see verses 26-27). Many white supremacists in the Southeastern United States identify the three sons of Noah as the progenitors of the races of the world- they identify Shem as the father of the Semites, Japheth as the ancestor of the white European race, and Ham, whose name is commonly interpreted as "burnt," is seen by many as the father of the black African race. In the Southeastern region of the United States, this passage was used to justify the enslavement of African Americans, who had been captured by European Americans and subsequently relocated to the United States:

> The heartless irreverence which Ham, the father of Canaan, displayed toward his eminent parent, whose piety had just saved him from the deluge, presented the immediate occasion for this remarkable prophecy; but the actual fulfillment was reserved for his posterity, after they had lost the knowledge of God, and became utterly polluted by the abominations of heathen idolatry. The Almighty foreseeing this total degradation of the race, ordained them to servitude of slavery under the descendants of Shem and Japheth, doubtless because he judged it to be their fittest condition. And all history proves how accurately this prediction has been accomplished, even to this present day.[4]

---

[4] John Henry Hopkins, *A Scriptural, Ecclesiastical, and Historical View of Slavery, from the Days of the Patriarch Abraham, to the Nineteenth Century* (New York: W.I. Pooley & Co.,

Conclusion and Implications for Ministry and Ecumenical Relations

This passage is still used to argue for the reinstitution of African American slavery among white supremacy groups in the United States, and it was also used to justify segregation and other forms of systematic oppression[5] in the southernmost regions of the Southeast United States prior to the Civil Rights movement of the 1960's. However, this is a severe misappropriation of this passage, as the ethnic groups of the world extend far beyond these three categories, and the Jews have equally been the targets of white supremacy groups in the Southeastern United States, such as the Ku Klux Klan. Consider the possible consequences of such an ideology, as reported by an African American abolitionist in the United States:

> I am filled with unutterable loathing when I contemplate the religious pomp and show, together with the horrible inconsistencies, which every where surround me. We have men-stealers for ministers, women-whippers for missionaries, and cradle-plunderers for church members.

Harper's Building, Franklin Square, 1864), 7/ Citation 2c-cited in "Biblical and Divine Justification for Slavery," The Making of America Project of University of Michigan and Cornell University, Posted by Martin December 2002, via *Internet*: <http://2thinkforums.org/anyboard/archive/16219.html.> Click on c2 for full text reference <http://www.hti.umich.edu/cgi/t/text/pageviewer...>: Homepage: "Making of America": <http://www.hti.umich.edu/cgi/t/text/text...>. Accessed May 13, 2005.

[5] Consider this statement from James D. Glasse, former Professor of Practical Theology and Director of Church and College Relations at Vanderbilt Divinity School, Vanderbilt University, 1967, "In the more rigorous form of left-wing, lower-middle-class, white Protestantism (which dominates the religious establishment) there is a principled aversion to religious symbolism and ceremonial: 'We don't have any creeds; we don't have any crosses; we don't wear any robes; we don't have any liturgies; we are just 'Christians'. And then at night, we put on robes and call each other kleagles and kluds, and burn a cross on somebody's lawn. The kind of thing we won't allow to happen in the daylight in the Church comes out at night behind the barn...It is the curious phenomenon whereby in a liquor election in the South, the preachers and the bootleggers are on the same side. And those of us who don't wear robes and burn crosses (and now are a little ashamed that our grandfathers did) were nonetheless raised on the same mythologies. We knew we were Christians, because we were not Jews. We knew we were Protestants because we were not Catholics. And we knew we were God's people because we were white." [James D. Glasse, "The Church in Mission in the Southeast" in *First Kentucky Faith and Order Conference: Louisville Presbyterian Theological Seminary, Louisville, Kentucky, May 15-18, 1967* ed. Paul A. Crow, Jr. (Lexington, Kentucky: Kentucky Council of Churches, 1967), 10-23: 14.]

The man who wields the blood-clotted cowskin during the week fills the pulpit on Sunday, and claims to be a minister of the meek and lowly Jesus. The man who robs me of my earnings at the end of the week meets me as a class-leader on Sunday morning, to show me the way of life, and the path of salvation. He who sells my sister, for purposes of prostitution, stands forth as the pious advocate of purity. He who proclaims it a religious duty to read the Bible denies me the right of learning to read the name of the God who made me…The slave auctioneer's bell and the church –going bell chime in with each other, and the bitter cries of the heart-broken slave are drowned in the religious shouts of his pious slave master.[6]

One who has been raised with this ideology must be given new options for a reinterpretation of this text, as no biblical text should ever be used as racist propaganda. The best option for reinterpreting this particular text is literary criticism, which identifies certain ancient Near Eastern literary genres utilized in the biblical texts for specific purposes. Using literary criticism, Biblical exegete Walter Brueggemann writes that in this passage, "…a *family narrative* is used to characterize *political realities* at some point in Israel's history."[7] In reading this narrative, one must take into consideration the fact that it was never meant to be a literal description of an event that happened to Noah and his sons. This is a narrative in which the author is trying to develop explanations for certain historical developments within the nation of Israel. The literary motif of the family narrative is used to explain from Israel's standpoint why certain conflicts have arisen among particular nations, as opposed to others.

This narrative occurs after the flood narrative, in which all of humankind, with the exception of Noah and his family, has been wiped off the face of the earth. According to this narrative, Noah and his three sons are left to propagate the human race. Shem represents the Semites, or the nation of Israel. The fact that the text mentions the son of Ham,

---

[6] Frederick Douglass, "Frederick Douglass on the Religion of Slaveholders" excerpt from the *Narrative of the Life of Frederick Douglass*, 1845 in *Christianity in America*, ed. Noll et al, 259-260.

[7] Walter Brueggemann, *Genesis* in *Interpretation: A Bible Commentary for Teaching and Preaching*, eds. James Luther Mays et al. (Atlanta, Georgia: John Knox Press, 1982), 90.

Conclusion and Implications for Ministry and Ecumenical Relations

instead of Ham himself, can be seen as a statement against the Canaanite lifestyle from the perspective of the Israelites during the time in which this narrative was written, as the Canaanites were always considered by Israel to be a sexually perverse group of people. Japheth is difficult to identify, but he most likely represents the Philistine nation, which has shared land with Israel at certain moments in its history.[8] Brueggemann writes, "This narrative is an opportunity to root in pre-history the power relations between Israel and Canaan and to justify it on theological grounds."[9]

One can also approach this text with a hermeneutic of suspicion, which examines this text from the perspective of the silenced voices that can be found both within and beyond the confines of the text. For instance, one might wonder why Noah chooses to curse only Canaan, when the text specifies that Ham has other sons (Genesis 9:25; 10:6). Such a question confirms Brueggemann's suggestion that the author expresses little concern about the actual circumstances surrounding Ham's behavior.[10] Instead, this text is used to symbolize a deeper problem- the hostility that exists between Israel and the Canaanites. Therefore, a symbolic reading of this text is also necessary in order to fully grasp the meaning of the text.

Whenever one further applies this interpretation to the condition of Israel during the time in which this text was written, one can assume that the nation of Israel, as represented by the drunken Noah, might have felt exposed and vulnerable at the moments in which it found itself surrounded by the Canaanites. Therefore, the authors might have used this narrative as an expression of their vulnerability in the presence of the Canaanite nation, which was the focus of the conquest in the book of Joshua.

Whenever one analyzes this passage from these various angles, one is forced to ask oneself questions concerning the ethical implications of such a passage: Is one ever truly justified in demonizing one group of people based on the reported actions a particular representative of that group? One must also ask if there is even a possibility that the individual ever committed such horrendous actions, or if such stories are being used to justify a particular reaction of the opposing group. This text challenges human beings to confront their own demons by asking difficult questions

---

[8] Brueggemann, *Genesis*, 89-92.
[9] Ibid., 90.
[10] *Ibid.*

concerning the actual perpetrators and victims of any given conflict. For one who is raised in a fundamentalist tradition in which certain groups are demonized on the basis of a so-called literal interpretation of scripture, one must ask if such a reading is truly "literal," or if it reflects the unidentified fears of that particular group of people.

Part II: Confronting Apocalyptic Enthusiasts from a Distant and More Recent Past

Whenever ministering to people who have been injured by extreme forms of apocalypticism, the ecumenically minded Christian needs to remain sensitive to the experiences of the person, realizing that if the person reports having gone through some traumatizing experience, that person is most likely not exaggerating. Within the American context, countless people have suffered in the hands of apocalyptic movements, with some popular examples being the Branch Davidians of Waco, Texas, the Heaven's Gate Cult, and the incident led by Jim Jones, in which the followers committed mass suicide by drinking Kool-Aid containing cyanide.

As mentioned previously, the author of this research underwent a similar experience, involving details, which have only been confronted in therapy sessions. In the same way, one should always be sensitive to the fact that for the person who has undergone such traumatic experiences, making the choice to reveal such experiences can be difficult, as the person may fear being misunderstood, classified as mentally unstable, or in worst-case scenarios, may fear the retribution of the perpetrators.

Instead of pronouncing judgment on these people, it would be helpful to listen to them and realize that there are contextual circumstances that encourage a person to develop fears surrounding the apocalypse. For a person who is raised within a fundamentalist tradition that is solely focused on the events of the eschaton, in which it is believed that God will pronounce judgment on all forms of evil, that person will most likely be inclined to view world events through such black-and-white theological lenses. As the state of the world becomes increasingly worse, this person will undoubtedly begin to wonder where she or he fits into the larger picture. There is always a religious group present to offer answers to such honest inquiries, regardless of whether the group-in-question is responding with

Conclusion and Implications for Ministry and Ecumenical Relations

good or evil intentions, or if the answers they provide produce positive or negative results.

Within the North American context, such fears of the apocalypse often reflect deep-seated fears of the American way of life being threatened, which includes the ideal of radical individualism, the democratic governance system, and the free-market economy. Often, such fears will be expressed through the use of popular apocalyptic symbols, such as the emergence of worldwide dictator, (the "Antichrist") or the imposition of a new economic system (communism, socialism). This interpretation of apocalyptic literature is not too far removed from that of so-called Third World apocalyptic theologies, except in the apocalyptic theologies of the so-called Third World, the identified evils are accordingly reversed:

> Making the biblical text sound even more relevant to modern Third World Christians, the evils described in Revelation are distinctively urban. Then as now, evil sets up its throne in cities. Brazilian scholar Gilberto da Silva Gorgulho remarks that 'The Book of Revelation is the favorite book of our popular communities. Here they find the encouragement they need in their struggle, and a criterion for the interpretation of official persecution in our society…The meaning of the church in history is rooted in the witness of the gospel before the state imperialism that destroys the people's life, looming as an ideal caricature of the Holy Trinity.' To a Christian living in a Third World dictatorship, the image of the government as Antichrist is not a bizarre religious fantasy, but a convincing piece of political analysis. Looking at Christianity as a planetary phenomenon, not merely a Western one, makes it possible to read the New Testament in quite the same way ever again. The Christianity we see through this exercise looks like a very exotic beast indeed, intriguing, exciting, and a little frightening.[11]

Whenever an ecumenically minded Christian is offering counsel to a former fundamentalist who has been injured by extreme forms of apocalypticism, the ecumenical person can reassure the former fundamentalist Christian that he or she is not "crazy" for having adopted

---

[11] Jenkins, *The Next Christendom*, 219-220. [Jenkins supplies a quotation from Gilberto da Silva Gorgulho, as he is originally quoted in Ruiz, "Biblical Interpretation," 86-87.]

such a belief system. Once any person feels that his or her way of life is threatened in any way, it is not uncommon for that person to seek a theological explanation for the suffering that one is either undergoing, or foresees oneself undergoing in the future. The former fundamentalist can find comfort in the realization that anyone, given the right conditions, can be driven to adopt such eschatological approaches.

Instead of judging the person for his or her past experiences, the ecumenically minded Christian should encourage the former fundamentalist to research the historical development of various historical and current apocalyptic movements within, and beyond, the United States, and to ask critical questions regarding the historical circumstances that gave rise to such a theology: such as the fears of the people at that moment, the actions of the government at that time, and the particular biblical texts to which the people turn for answers.

After this critical analysis, the ecumenical Christian can encourage the former fundamentalist to draw parallels between the historical group-in-question and the group from which the individual emerged. This will encourage the former fundamentalist to ask critical questions pertaining to the circumstances that drove her or him to embrace such a belief system. Such an exercise will prove to be healing in the life of the former fundamentalist, who is most likely blaming oneself for having adopted such apocalyptic beliefs. This critical evaluation will help the former fundamentalist realize that she or he is not at fault adopting certain religious beliefs in the past, and such a realization will make the person stronger and more self-assured for dealing with similar situations in the future.

Part III: Christological Issues

For one who is struggling to emerge from a fundamentalist tradition, perhaps one of the greatest obstacles in doing so is dealing with questions of Christology. Any fundamentalist group that speaks of Jesus as the physical manifestation of a loving deity who was willing to come down to earth and die for the sins of humanity, but at the same time, places an even stronger emphasis on the impending wrath and judgment of God, which will be fully manifested in the second coming of Christ, sends

Conclusion and Implications for Ministry and Ecumenical Relations

contradictory messages to its members concerning the true nature of God, or the person Jesus of Nazareth. Such an approach to Christological issues can often strike fear in the heart of the fundamentalist, who sincerely desires to believe that God sent Jesus to die for him or her, but is simultaneously afraid that God/Jesus do not see her or him as worthy to receive salvation in the end.

In the North American context, rapture films, such as *A Thief in the Night*, and radio shows such as "The Prophecy Club," serve to further validate such fears. There is a scene in *A Distant Thunder*, in which Patty Myers, after having been captured by UNITE, is recounting events in her life prior to the rapture. She recalls a moment in which she and her devout Christian grandmother were discussing the events of the eschaton while baking cookies together. Patty, herself a lifelong churchgoer from a more liberal denomination, relates to her grandmother that she does not understand how God can allow such horrific events to occur if God is love. Her grandmother responds by saying that God is so holy that God cannot look upon sin. Nevertheless, Patty is confused by the claims of her grandmother, and when she finally does find herself left here on earth after the rapture, she expresses anger towards God for having left her behind. The deity who her former pastor proclaimed as loving proved itself to be a merciless and bloodthirsty ethereal tyrant.[12]

There are many aspects of this theology that cannot be adequately addressed here, but the simple problem is that this theological perspective presents Jesus as aligned with, if not equal to, this self-contradictory God. If Jesus truly is the self-manifestation of this uncompromising deity who supposedly died for all humankind, then this means that Jesus, who cannot look on sin, can be highly selective as to whom he will or will not redeem. This causes serious problems in the life of the struggling fundamentalist, who realizes that she or he will never measure up to the impossible standards of God, even if the church does claim that grace is available for everyone who asks.

Such problems call for a further inquiry into the actual nature of the person Jesus of Nazareth, who is called the Christ. If Jesus of Nazareth is the same person as the Jesus who both died on the cross and is believed

---

[12] Mark IV Productions, *A Distant Thunder* (1977). It is interesting to note that in the movie, Patty's minister is also left on earth after the rapture.

by many Christians to be seated on the right hand of God, then there must be some level of continuity present between the person of Jesus and the Jesus who is called the Christ. This further compels one to examine the life of Jesus of Nazareth, and to ask if he was really the condemning, uncompromising person that many fundamentalists portray him as.

Whenever one truly examines the life of Jesus of Nazareth, as it is recorded in the Synoptic Gospels, he is presented as having displayed unlimited compassion towards the marginalized who are in need of God's love the most (cf. Matthew 8:1-4; 28-34, 9:18-33, Mark 1:21-28; 32-34, 2:1-12, 3:1-6, 5:21-43, 10: 13-16, Luke 7:1-17; 36-50, 8:26-48, 18:35-43, 19:1-10, 21: 1-4). At times, Jesus did display anger and condemnation towards people, but ironically, the two main groups of people that he was so quick to challenge were the Pharisees and Sadducees, who were the religious officials that were working in close connection with the oppressive Roman government at that time (cf. Matthew 16:1-6, 23, Mark 2:15-28, 7:13, 10:9, Luke 6:1-11, 7: 36-50, 11:37-44, 12:1-3, 15, 20). Jesus condemns these people due to their self-righteous attitudes. However, Jesus is more than willing to shower compassion upon the people who realize that they need it the most and who are not ashamed to admit that they are unworthy to receive it.

In his report, "A Case for Pro-Active Spirituality: A Spiritual Vision for the Dialogue of Religions," Swami Agnivesh, a political activist for the abolishment of the caste system in India and an active participant in an ongoing United Nations forum on spirituality, writes:

> I have often wondered why Jesus said that the prostitutes would enter the Kingdom before the Pharisees and Sadducees. Could it be that they have greater freedom in meeting people and are richer through their shared experiences? The religious frigidity of the priestly class was anathema to Jesus, who stood for a robust celebration of life. Somehow, for a person like me, it is difficult to visualize Jesus of Nazareth inside a church, except perhaps in the form of an idol set up for cosmetic considerations.[13]

---

[13] Swami Agnivesh, "A Case for Pro-Active Spirituality: A Spiritual Vision for the Dialogue of Religions," Unpublished Work: A report given to the author of this research project by Swami Agnivesh at the Ecumenical Institute Bossey in May, 2005.

Conclusion and Implications for Ministry and Ecumenical Relations

If Jesus of Nazareth, as the earthly representative of God on earth, devotes much of his earthly ministry proclaiming life to the lifeless, health to the sick, forgiveness to the condemned, and hope to the hopeless, one must ask why so many fundamentalist Christians within the United States focus almost exclusively on the impending wrath of God, as it is unleashed through the Second Coming of Jesus the Christ.

The former fundamentalist will undoubtedly ask such questions, and she or he is completely justified in doing so. Therefore, the ecumenically minded Christian must be prepared to encounter such questions, as they will be asked. One suggestion for the ecumenically minded Christian who is addressing such questions is to refer to the life of Jesus, as it is recorded in the Synoptic Gospels, and to ask the former fundamentalist questions as to who Jesus really directs his anger towards, as opposed to those to whom he pronounces healing and wholeness. Once the former fundamentalist begins to critically examine the life of Jesus, he or she will begin to see that he only pronounced condemnation on those who already saw themselves as righteous, while at the same time, openly supporting systems of injustice and oppression. Such a realization will encourage the former fundamentalist to follow the example of Jesus of Nazareth, who was actively engaged in the struggle for justice in the midst of an unjust world, and therefore, calls all true believers to do the same, no matter the cost.

Using the words of Swami Agnivesh, many fundamentalist churches in the United States do indeed make Jesus of Nazareth "…in the form of an idol set up for cosmetic considerations."[14] For many sincere Protestant fundamentalist Christians in the U.S., Jesus is presented as nothing more than a static character- an "idol"[15]- who while somehow being human, lives by impossible standards, is omniscient, and yet, somehow expects human beings to either emulate his life or be subjected to God's unrelenting wrath. Such an understanding is not too far removed from that of the Docetists, who were considered heretical during the time of the early Church. The Docetists believed that Jesus only appeared to be human; that he never truly endured the struggles of humanity. Such fixed images of Jesus portray Jesus as a rather shadowy and unapproachable figure. Therefore, it should not come as a surprise that many former fundamentalists from the United

---

[14] Swami Agnivesh, "A Case for Pro-Active Spirituality."
[15] *Ibid.*

States are afraid of the popular images of Jesus returning to earth in the clouds to receive his people.

Part IV: Developing a Responsible Eschatology

One of the most difficult tasks of a former fundamentalist is to restructure one's understanding of eschatology in a responsible manner, which takes into account both the spiritual and ethical dimensions of prophetic and apocalyptic literature. Although it must be acknowledged that certain religious groups take eschatological interpretation too far, the more ecumenical denominations can learn something important from these fundamentalist groups, in that one cannot simply ignore or over spiritualize the apocalyptic and prophetic texts, because the state of the world is not improving, and many Christians are, indeed, being imprisoned or giving their lives for the sake of promoting justice in the world.

The former fundamentalist, who might not be ready to completely abandon an eschatological approach to reality, but at the same time, realizes the difficulties that present themselves in the eschatology of his or her former denomination, may approach an ecumenically minded Christian with questions concerning how to deal with difficult apocalyptic passages, such as the apocalyptic imagery surrounding the Great Tribulation, as recorded in the book of Revelation. When dealing with such questions, it is important to point out to the former fundamentalist that one does not have to know all the answers to such difficult questions; Christians have been baffled by the apocalyptic imagery of Revelation and similar apocalyptic texts for centuries. However, the ecumenical Christian can offer to work with the former fundamentalist in seeking responsible answers to such questions.

One suggestion for approaching the difficult issue of the Great Tribulation is to ask the inquirer what he or she thinks concerning certain apocalyptic images: the Antichrist, the "Mark of the Beast," or the "Whore of Babylon." Next, one should ask the former fundamentalist if she or he sees any modern examples in the current world that could correspond to these images. When doing so, remind him or her about the evils of this world against which Jesus spoke, mainly the religious systems that worked hand-in-hand with the government in order to justify oppression.

Conclusion and Implications for Ministry and Ecumenical Relations

Also ask the former fundamentalist questions concerning the issues that the prophets of the Hebrew Scriptures decried within their respective societies. If the former fundamentalist answers these questions responsibly, encourage her or him to draw parallels between the evils of the apocalyptic and prophetic texts and the evils of modern society. Consequently, she or he will now have a more ample picture concerning types of evils that are condemned in such biblical texts.

During a recent class trip to Rome in February 2005 with the Graduate School of the Ecumenical Institute Bossey, the author of this research project saw an icon depicting "The Great Tribulation"[16] in Basilica di San Bartolomeo that was dedicated to the Christian martyrs over the centuries. This icon depicts groups of people from all over the world being persecuted and martyred for their faith. One prominent example contained within this icon is Archbishop Oscar Romero, who died in the struggle for the liberation of his people in El Salvador. At the top of the icon, the saints who have been martyred for their faith are depicted as wearing white robes and holding palm branches as they surround Jesus and the Holy Virgin. Two small children are even featured among these heavenly martyrs.

This icon, which the author first assumed would be frightening, actually provided a sense of comfort, as it was not focused on a predicted future moment in which people who accepted Christ after the rapture would be captured and beheaded. Instead, it depicted modern Christians fighting for justice in a world that denies basic rights to innocent people. Instead of provoking fear, this icon provokes the onlooker to fight for justice in the world; reminding the Christian of God's presence, not only in the midst of the suffering of the martyr, but in the suffering of the people for whom the martyr advocates justice. The martyrs depicted in this icon represent the ongoing struggle for the ideals of the Reign of God in the world, the ideals for which Jesus was killed; ideals that call humanity to a higher reality.

For the person who has been wounded by extreme forms of apocalypticism, such as the author of this research project, this icon can offer healing and comfort, as it reassures the onlooker that one is never alone in the struggle for justice. Jesus himself fought for the ideals of

---

[16] Representation of Icon: "Attraverso La Grande Tribolazione" Comunita Di Sant'Egidio, Icona dei "Nuovi Martiri" (Roma: Basilica di San Bartolomeo) all'Isola Tiberina.

the Reign of God in his everyday earthly existence, and his exemplary life serves as a calling for all to join him in doing the same, regardless of denomination or religion. The struggles for justice are never in vain, as they advocate God's vision of abundant life for all. For the former Protestant fundamentalist in the United States of America, this icon, and any other relevant symbols which may speak to the individual, can serve to call one to reach beyond one's geographical, cultural, and ideological barriers in order to join followers of Christ all over the world in the ongoing struggle for the integrity of all people as joint heirs of God's vision of justice in the world.

A Ministry of Reconciliation: Going Beyond Issues of Theology to the Heart of the Matter

So far, this research has concerned itself primarily with issues of doctrine, such as biblical interpretation, eschatology, and Christological topics. However, helping one merely work through issues of doctrine is not enough to truly promote healing in the life of the former fundamentalist. One must also concentrate on the spiritual dimension of healing within the life of the individual, and although confronting one's previous notions of God is a vital part of spiritual healing, the spiritual dimension of healing must reach much deeper- to the depths of one's being.

In his essay, "Unraveling A 'Complex Reality': Six Elements of Mission," Stephen Bevans identities six key elements of mission: (1) witness and proclamation, (2) liturgy, prayer, and contemplation, (3) justice, peace, and the integrity of creation, (4) interreligious/secular dialogue, (5) inculturation, and (6) reconciliation.[17] While the first five elements of mission cannot be ignored, the final element is the most crucial for a Christian who is emerging from the influence of fundamentalism. It is common for one who has come out of a fundamentalist tradition to harbor bitterness against one's former denomination, and for those people who have been extremely hurt by such an experience, the process of recovery

---

[17] Stephen Bevans, "Unraveling A 'Complex Reality': Six Elements of Mission," Paper Presented in Missiology, Ecumenical Institute Bossey, by Dr. Elizabeth S. Tapia, 26 October 2004.

Conclusion and Implications for Ministry and Ecumenical Relations

may take years, perhaps even a lifetime. Therefore, ecumenically minded Christians need to develop awareness, sensitivity and patience with those to whom they are offering counsel. By expressing solidarity with the injured party, the ecumenically minded Christian shows the former fundamentalist that he or she takes the struggles of that person seriously. In this way, the ecumenically minded Christian can indeed serve as a vital support system for the former fundamentalist Christian, displaying firsthand the healing and sustaining power of God's unconditional love, and in doing so, showing the person that reconciliation is possible.[18]

The first step in the process of healing from fundamentalism is to achieve reconciliation within oneself. It is important for the one who is offering counsel to a former fundamentalist to remind the person that one should never allow the future to be plagued by the events of the past. One must never forget that at one time or another, every human being makes errors of judgment, due to a variety of circumstantial reasons and personal limitations. This is why it is important for ecumenically minded Christian to assist the former fundamentalist in the process of a recovery and healing of memories.[19] If addressed in a proper way, painful memories can be used to become "…the building blocks of a different kind of future."[20]

Once again, it is important to remember that it takes time and patience for the healing process to occur, so the one who is assisting the former fundamentalist should exercise patience when supporting one through this difficult process of recovering and healing memories. However, since memories are integral to one's identity as a human being,[21] it is important

---

[18] Jacques Matthey, ed. Commission on World Mission and Evangelism, World Council of Churches, "Statement on Mission as Reconcilation" in WCC Conference on World Mission and Evangelism: *Come Holy Spirit- Heal and Reconcile: "Called in Christ to be Reconciling and Healing Communities, Athens, Greece, 9-16 May 2005, Preparatory Paper No. 4"* (Prepared March 2004: 4: p. 11). This report states, "Accompanying victims so that they can come free from traumatic memories is an important task of those who work for reconciliation."

[19] CWME, "Statement on Mission as Reconciliation," Preparatory Paper No. 4: pp. 11-12.

[20] Ibid., No. 4 p. 11.

[21] *Ibid.*, According to this report, "Memories are not just about the past. They are the basis for identity. *How* we remember the past is both the basis for how we will live and relate to one another in the present, and how we will envision the future. For that reason, memory is central to the process of healing and reconciliation."

for the one who is offering counsel to the victim to encourage the victim to recall and address any painful memories with authority and conviction, realizing that if one ignores these memories, they will return to haunt one in the future. The act of recalling painful memories helps one to place them into their proper perspective and to consider ways to transform them into something positive. According to CWME Preparatory Paper No. 4, "To heal memories means that they lose their toxic quality. When that happens, memories do not hold us hostage to the past, but empower us to create a future where the wrongdoing of the past cannot happen again."[22]

After one confronts the painful events of the past, it is important for the ecumenically minded Christian to begin to find ways to promote reconciliation and forgiveness between the former fundamentalist and the church of her or his past. While it may be impossible in the earlier stages of the healing process for the wounded one to face the people from one's past, it is important for both the ecumenically minded Christian and the former fundamentalist to keep in mind that the struggles of the former fundamentalist Christian is symptomatic of a deeper problem: the brokenness of the Body of Christ.

For a former fundamentalist Christian who knows the mindset of fundamentalist Christianity and is turning to the ecumenically minded denomination in search of new ways of affirming one's commitment to Christ, this person would be the ideal candidate to serve as a mediator, or a point of reconciliation, between the two traditions in the future. However, the former fundamentalist cannot perform this task alone, as he or she might not yet be strong enough to do so. This is where the ecumenically minded Christian, as an agent of God's mission of reconciliation, must come to the aide of former fundamentalist in seeking to promote reconciliation between the two denominations. It is important to remember, "If churches are not able to reconcile one with the other, they are failing to gospel call and will lack credibility in witness." [23]

The first step in this process of reconciliation is for the ecumenically minded Christian to carefully assess the shortcomings within his or her own denomination. While the denomination-in-question might claim to be ecumenically oriented, there is always the possibility that this

---

[22] *Ibid.*
[23] CWME, "Statement on Mission as Reconciliation," Preparatory Paper No. 4: p. 15.

Conclusion and Implications for Ministry and Ecumenical Relations

denomination has never attempted to reach out to the fundamentalist churches in the area, most likely out of fear. It is important, in helping the former fundamentalist confront the issues of his or her past, to speak openly and honestly about the shortcomings that exist within one's own denomination, so that the former fundamentalist will not find oneself disillusioned with the new denomination within the upcoming years and eventually abandon Christianity altogether. It is important to remind the former fundamentalist that while the Church does claim to be the visible representative of Christ on earth, the Church is limited by its own mortality: "Any credible mission by the church has to begin with the confession that not all of her mission has been a reflection of the mission which God has intended and which Godself carries out in the world through the work and ministry of the Holy Spirit (*missio Dei*)."[24] All denominations, regardless of their best intentions, are "broken icons"[25] of the reconciling work of God in the world.

After having worked extensively with the former fundamentalist in dealing with his or her individual theological and spiritual concerns, the ecumenically minded Christian can offer to accompany the former fundamentalist in a conference with her or his former pastor and assist the person in addressing these issues of concern. One must be careful in doing so, especially if the former fundamentalist remains traumatized from certain experiences within that church. However, if an extra person who is aware of the past struggles of the other person offers to serve as a mediator between the former fundamentalist and the pastor, the former fundamentalist will find strength in the extra support.

When meeting with the fundamentalist pastor, both the former fundamentalist and the one who is offering counsel should remain patient and refrain from being accusatory, realizing that the fundamentalist pastor is most likely not prepared for such an encounter and may not even be aware of the pain that this person has undergone. The first two parties should talk openly with the pastor, expressing their concerns and their desire for reconciliation as fellow members of the Body of Christ. The participants in this meeting should begin with prayer, surrendering

---

[24] CWME, "Statement on Mission as Reconciliation," Preparatory Paper No. 4: p. 15.
[25] Dr. Martin Robra, Interdisciplinary Seminar: Mission and Evangelism/Social Ethics, Ecumenical Institute Bossey, May 2005.

this time to the transforming power of the Holy Spirit. As Preparatory Paper No. 4 for the 2005 CWME Conference states, "The spirituality of reconciliation is one of humility and self-emptying (*kenosis*; Phil. 2:7), and at the same time an experience of the Holy Spirit's sanctifying and transforming power."[26] In agreeing to begin this session with prayer, all involved parties will be reassured that this meeting is not meant to be a hostile confrontation, and they will begin the session in the right frame of mind.

Next, the former fundamentalist should proceed to speak honestly about his or her struggles within the fundamentalist church, while making it clear that she or he still desires to remain a Christian. The fundamentalist pastor should be made aware of the various reasons that people are leaving his (or her) church.[27] The former member should then take this opportunity to offer suggestions for how to address these concerns in the future. For instance, if the main concern is the overemphasis of the denomination on the second coming of Christ, the former member could suggest for the pastor to pay more attention to the life and ministry of Jesus while he was on earth. If the former member is concerned that the church leaders are scaring people (or in more extreme cases, children or youth) into making decisions for Christ, either through "hellfire and brimstone" sermons or apocalyptic films, such as *A Thief in the Night*, the former member could suggest that the pastor focus more on the love of God as revealed in the life and death of Jesus of Nazareth. In regards to the struggles with denominational claims of biblical inerrancy, the former member could show the pastor a passage that he or she feels could be interpreted in other ways and offer new possibilities for approaching this passage.

There are appropriate ways to approach the fundamentalist pastor without appearing to be too liberal minded or unbiblical. The former fundamentalist, who is in a state of transition between the two denominations and knows the rhetoric of the fundamentalist tradition, is the best person to address these concerns to the pastor and can find ways to do so in a way that is not perceived by the pastor to be too challenging or threatening to the tradition. The ecumenically minded Christian, as a

---

[26] CWME, "Statement on Mission as Reconciliation," Preparatory Paper No. 4: p. 16.

[27] Most fundamentalist pastors are male, although there are rare exceptions.

Conclusion and Implications for Ministry and Ecumenical Relations

representative of the more moderate or liberal tradition, can be present as a mediator in order to make sure that the meeting does not become too confrontational or emotionally-charged.

If this meeting is handled in a responsible way, it can become productive, not only for the parties involved, but for the future of that fundamentalist church and denomination. Such a meeting can also be beneficial to the other (ecumenical) denomination, as honest dialogue so often sheds light on the shortcomings and limitations of all parties involved. If all the parties involved in this discussion are open to the work of the Holy Spirit, this type of meeting can also open doors to future ecumenical relations between the two denominations, offering healing and reconciliation to all who are within the reach of its influence.

Final Synopsis and Recommendations for Further Study

The purpose of this thesis has been to conduct a textual analysis of the various documents that from various bilateral dialogues held among evangelicals and non-evangelicals in order to determine if any conclusions could be reached as to how ecumenically minded Christians could more effectively respond to the spiritual and theological concerns of former fundamentalists in the United States, especially regarding the issues of biblical interpretation and eschatology. Through conducting a textual analysis of the following documents: *Lutherans and Adventists in Conversation: Report and Papers Presented 1994-1998, Baptists and Reformed in Dialogue: Documents from the Conversations Sponsored by the World Alliance of Reformed Churches and the Baptist World Alliance, Consultation with Pentecostals in the Americas*, and *The World Council of Churches/Seventh-Day Adventist Conversations and Their Significance*, the author reached a variety of conclusions that can be applied to answer the question of how ecumenically minded Christians can more effectively minister to the spiritual and theological concerns of former Protestant fundamentalists. The main conclusions which were reached within this textual analysis included: (1) one's life experience always influences scriptural interpretation on some level, (2) most denominations can report a time in which certain members of their tradition were concerned with apocalyptic issues, (3) most Christians acknowledge that Jesus of Nazareth, remains the center of all eschatological concerns, (4) all Christians need to develop a responsible approach to eschatological matters, paying equal attention to the "signs of the times" and the ethical dimension of apocalyptic and prophetic texts.

The next section further developed the aforementioned conclusions in order to offer practical suggestions on how ecumenically minded Christians could more effectively minister to the spiritual and theological concerns of former Protestant fundamentalists within the United States. One of the important practical suggestions within this section included encouraging the former fundamentalist to look beyond his or her immediate religious and geographical contexts for other possible approaches to scripture and apocalyptic concerns. In the end, this research goes beyond dealing with mere theological issues to addressing issues of healing and reconciliation, which reaches beyond the life of the former fundamentalist, as it promotes dialogue and reconciliation among previously estranged members of the Body of Christ.

This research leads to a number of topics that could be further explored and developed in a future study. The first topic that requires further attention involves the question of how to develop a responsible eschatology. This issue has only been examined on a surface level within this thesis, and it deserves to be given more consideration in the future.[28] The prophetic and apocalyptic texts are either overused or almost completely ignored among many modern Christians, and the Church of today needs to find healthy and responsible ways to examine these texts anew, so that the prophetic voice of the Church will be strengthened in the midst of a world that is plagued with manifold injustices.

The second issue that should be explored more in depth is how a former fundamentalist might more effectively serve as a mediator between the former and current denominations. While agreeing to meet and share concerns with one's former pastor is a positive step in this direction, after this step is taken, there must be other ways in which the former fundamentalist can continue the task of bridging the gaps between the

---

[28] Additional credit must be given for this statement to the Rev. Dr. Thomas F. Best of the Faith and Order Commission of the World Council of Churches, as a similar suggestion was made during a Plenary Lecture delivered at the Ecumenical Institute Bossey in the Fall Semester of 2004.

Conclusion and Implications for Ministry and Ecumenical Relations

two ecclesial traditions. As one who stands between the two traditions, the former fundamentalist would be the ideal candidate for this task. This is an issue that calls for further study, as reconciliation between fundamentalists and ecumenically minded Christians is indispensable to the unity of the Body of Christ.

Finally, it would be important to explore more in depth the role of the ecumenically minded Christian in this ministry of reconciliation among fundamentalist and non-fundamentalist denominations. While it is important for the ecumenically minded Christian to assist the former fundamentalist Christian in dealing with certain theological and spiritual issues of concern and to serve as a mediator between her or his previous pastor, it would be important to explore more ways in which the ecumenically minded Christian could aide in this crucial ministry of healing and reconciliation, and in doing so, further the mission of God on earth.

Bibliography

Articles:
Matthey, Jacques, ed. *International Review of Mission*, Volume 92: No. 365. Geneva: WCC Publications, 2003.

Secretariat for Promoting Christian Unity, The. *The Secretariat for Promoting Christian Unity: Information Service*. English Edition: No. 35; Volumes III-IV. Vatican City State: Secretariat for Christian Unity, 1977.

World Council of Churches. Department of Reconstruction and Interchurch Aid. "Evangelism in North America" *Quarry* Article, No. 32b, WCC Archives. Geneva, Switzerland: World Council of Churches, 1948.

Books:
Barr, James. *Escaping From Fundamentalism*. London: SCM Press, 1984.

Coleman, Simon. *The Globalization of Charismatic Christianity: Spreading the Gospel of Prosperity*. Cambridge, U.K.: The Press Syndicate of Cambridge University Press, 2000.

Dirks, Lee E. *Religion in Action: How America's Faiths Are Meeting New Challenges*. Newsbook. Silver Spring, Maryland: The National Observer, 1965.

Du Plessis, David J. *The Spirit Bade Me Go: The Astounding Move of God in the Denominational Churches*. Revised and Enlarged. Oakland: California: David J. Du Plessis, n.d.

Fanshaw, D., printer, *Nevin's Practical Thoughts & Popery*. Evangelical Family Library, author William Nevins. New York: American Tract Society, 1836.

Feder, Don. *Who's Afraid of the Religious Right?* Washington, DC: Regnery Publishing, Inc, 1996.

Fey, Harold E., ed. *How My Mind Has Changed: Thirteen Distinguished Religious Thinkers Access the Impact of the Last Decades on Their Lives and Thought*. Living Age Books,

Bibliography

Consulting Editor Marvin P. Halverson. Cleveland Ohio/New York: Meridian Books, The World Publishing Company, 1961.

Fisher, Wallace E. *The Affable Enemy: Correspondence with a Christian Dropout.* Nashville, Tennessee /New York: Abingdon Press, 1970.

Graham, Billy. *Peace With God.* Garden City, New York: Doubleday and Company, Inc., 1953.

Green, Joel B. and Mark Baker. *Recovering the Scandal of the Cross: Atonement in New Testament and Contemporary Contexts.* Illinois: Intervarsity Press, 2000.

Gritsch, Eric W. *Born Againism: Perspectives on a Movement.* Philadelphia: Fortress Press, 1982.

Harding, Susan Friend. *The Book of Jerry Falwell: Fundamentalist Language and Politics.* Princeton: Princeton University Press, 2000.

James, Janet Wilson, ed. *Women in American Religion.* Philadelphia, Pennsylvania: University of Pennsylvania Press, 1980.

Jenkins, Philip. *The Next Christendom: The Coming of Global Christianity.* New York: Oxford University Press, 2002.

Lindsey, Hal. *The Late Great Planet Earth*, with C.C. Carlson. Grand Rapids: Michigan: Zondervan, 1970.

_____. *Satan is Alive and Well on Planet Earth*, with C.C. Carlson. Grand Rapids, Michigan: Zondervan Publishing House, 1972.

Luz, Ulrich. *New Testament Theology: The Theology of the Gospel of Matthew,* eds. James D. G. Dunn, et al, trans. J. Bradford Robinson. Great Britain: Cambridge University Press, 1993.

Marsden, George M. *Fundamentalism and American Culture: The Shaping of Twentieth Century Evangelicalism, 1870-1925.* New York/Oxford: Oxford University Press, 1980.

Melton, J. Gordon, and Robert L. Moore. *The Cult Experience: Responding to the New Religious Pluralism.* New York: The Pilgrim Press, 1986.

Noll, Mark A., et al., eds. *Christianity in America: A Handbook.* A Lion Book. Grand Rapids Michigan: William B. Eerdmans Publishing Company, 1983.

Rolston, H. *Thessalonians to Philemon.* London: SCM Press Ltd., 1963.

Rosenburg, Ellen M. *The Southern Baptists: A Subculture in Transition.* Knoxville, TN: The University of Tennessee Press, 1989.

Rosio, Bob. *The Culture War in America: A Society in Chaos.* Lafayette, Louisiana: Huntington House Publishers, 1995.

Russell, D.S. *Between the Testaments.* London: SCM Press Ltd., 1960.

Sandeen, Ernest R. *The Roots of Fundamentalism: British and American Millenarianism, 1800-1930.* Grand Rapids: Baker Book House, 1978.

Sargant, William. *Battle for the Mind: A Physiology of Conversion and Brain-washing.* London: William Heinemann Ltd., 1957.

Spong, John Shelby. *Rescuing the Bible from Fundamentalism: A Bishop Rethinks the Meaning of Scripture.* New York: HarperCollins Publishers, 1991.

Wilcox, Clyde. *Onward Christian Soldiers?: The Religious Right in American Politics.* Dilemmas in American Politics: Series Editor, L. Sandy Maisel. Boulder, Colorado/ Oxford, United Kingdom: Westview Press, 1996.

Wood, Jr., James E. ed. *Baptists and the American Experience.* Valley Forge, Pennsylvania: Judson Press, 1976.

Documents and Reports:

Agnivesh, Swami. "A Case for Pro-Active Spirituality: A Vision for the Dialogue of Religions": Unpublished Work. Report Given to the author at the Ecumenical Institute Bossey, May 2005.

Bevans, Stephen, "Unraveling A 'Complex Reality': Six Elements of Mission," Paper Presented in Missiology, Ecumenical Institute Bossey, by Dr. Elizabeth S. Tapia, October 2004.

Burke, David G., ed. *The Church and American Civil Religion: A Report from the USA Lutheran World Federation Study Group, 1984-1985.* New York: Lutheran World Ministries, 1986.

Cottrell, Raymond F. *The Eschaton: A Seventh-day Adventist Perspective. Report Prepared for the Second Ecumenical Consultation Between Select Representatives of the World Council of Churches and Seventh-Day Adventists at Andrews University, Berrien Springs, Michigan March 4 and 5, 1970.* Washington, D.C.: Review and Herald Publishing Company, 1970.

Crow, Jr. Paul A., ed. *First Kentucky Faith and Order Conference, Louisville Presbyterian Theological Seminary, Louisville, Kentucky, May 15-18, 1967.* Lexington, Kentucky: Kentucky Council of Churches, 1967.

General Conference of Seventh-Day Adventists and the Lutheran World Federation. *Lutherans & Adventists in Conversation: Report and Papers Presented 1994-1998.* Silver Springs, Maryland, USA: General Conference of Seventh-day Adventists and Geneva, Switzerland: Lutheran World Federation, 2000.

Handspicker, M.B. and Lukas Vischer, eds. *An Ecumenical Exercise: The Southern Baptist Convention, The Seventh-Day Adventist Church, The Kimbanguist Church in the Congo, The Pentecostal Movement in Europe.* Faith and Order Paper No. 49. Geneva: World Council of Churches, 1967.

Roebeck, Jr. Cecil M. "The Assemblies of God and Ecumenical Cooperation." Fuller Theological Seminary, Pasadena, California: n.d.

van Beek, Huibert, ed. *Consultation with Pentecostals in the Americas: San Jose, Costa Rica 4-8 June 1996.* Office of Church and Ecumenical Relations, Geneva: World Council of Churches, n.d.

Wilson, H.S., ed. *Christian Fundamentalism: The Papers and Findings of the WARC, LWF, PCPCU Consulation, 22 to 26 February 1993.* Geneva: World Alliance of Reformed Churches, 1994.

World Alliance of Reformed Churches. *Baptists and Reformed in Dialogue: Documents from the Conversations Sponsored by the World Alliance of Reformed Churches and the Baptist World Alliance.* Geneva: World Alliance of Reformed Churches, 1984.

Bibliography

World Council of Churches. *The World Council of Churches/Seventh-Day Adventist Conversations and their Significance*, Faith and Order Papers No. 55. Reprinted from *The Ecumenical Review* Vol. XXII No. 2-April 1970. Switzerland: n.d.

_____. *The World Council of Churches/Seventh-Day Adventist Conversations: Meetings in 1970-1971*, Faith and Order Paper No. 62/Reprinted from *The Ecumenical Review* Vol. XXIV No. 2- April 1972. Switzerland, n.d.

_____. *So Much in Common: Documents of Interest in the Conversations Between the World Council of Churches and the Seventh-day Adventist Church*. Geneva: World Council of Churches, 1973.

_____. *Consultation with Pentecostal Churches: Lima, Peru 14-19 November 1994*, Office of Church and Ecumenical Relations. Bialystok: Poland: Orthdruk Orthodox Printing House, n.d.

_____. WCC Conference on World Mission and Evangelism. *Come Holy Spirit-Heal and Reconcile: Called in Christ to be Reconciling and Healing Communities,* Athens, Greece, 9-16 May 2005: Preparatory Papers: 3-4.

Films:

Mark IV Productions. *A Thief in the Night*. Director Donald W. Thompson. Writing Credits: Russell S. Doughten, Jr., and Jim Grant Des Moines, Iowa: 1972.

_____. *A Distant Thunder*. Director Donald W. Thompson. Screenplay and Story: Russell S. Doughten, Jr. Des Moines, Iowa: 1977.

_____. *Image of the Beast*. Director Donald W. Thompson. Writing Credits: Russell S. Doughten, Jr. and Donald W. Thompson. Des Moines, Iowa: 1981.

_____. *The Prodigal Planet*. Director Donald W. Thompson. Screenplay and Story: Russell S. Doughten, Jr. Des Moines, Iowa: 1983.

Reference Materials:

Brasher, Brenda E., ed. *Encyclopedia of Fundamentalism*. Religion & Society: A Berkshire Reference Book. New York/London: Routledge, 2001.

Brueggemann, Walter. *Genesis* in *Interpretation: A Biblical Commentary for Teaching and Preaching,* series eds. James Luther Mays et al. Atlanta, Georgia: John Knox Press, 1982.

Cross, Frank Moore, ed. *Daniel: A Commentary on the Book of Daniel* by John J. Collins (with an essay "The Influence of Daniel on the New Testament," by Adela Yarbro Collins) Hermeneia- A Critical and Historical Commentary on the Bible. Minneapolis: Fortress Press, 1993.

Geaves, Ron, ed. *Continuum Glossary of Religious Terms*. London/New York: Continuum, 2002.

Landes, Richard A., ed. *Encyclopedia of Millenialism and Millennial Movements*. Religion and Society: A Berkshire Reference Work. New York/London: Routledge, 2000.

McBrien, Richard P., et al, eds. *The Harpercollins Encyclopedia of Catholicism*. San Francisco: HarperCollins Publishers, 1995.

Websites:

Editor(s) Unknown, "Visit Sullivan County, Tennessee: Christian Fundamentalism Exposed," via *Internet*, Updated February 12, 2003: <http://sullivan-county.com/news/>.

Hein, Anton, ed. "Apologetics Index" (Research Resource), via *Internet*, August 23, 2004: Homepage: <http://www.apologeticsindex.org/>.

Hughes, Phil. "The Telson Spur: Field Nodes – Paths 7," via *Internet*. British Columbia: Canada, February 21, 2005: Homepage: <http://www.snark.org/~pjhughes/ate3.htm>.

Hurricane Electronic Internet Services. "Adult Christianity" via *Internet*, 1995-2005: Homepage: <http://www.jesus21.com/index.php?s=default>.

Internet Movie Database Inc., an amazon.com company, via *Internet*, 1990-2004: Homepage: <http://imdb.com/title>.

Legal Information Institute: Cornell University, via *Internet*, Ithaca: NY: Startup Date 1992: Homepage: <http://www.law.cornell.edu/>.

Prophecy Club, The. The Prophecy Club Home Page. Founders, Stan and Leslie Johnson, Topeka, Kansas: 2004, via *Internet*: Homepage: <http://www.prophecyclub.com/index.htm>.

SDA Global. "Ellen White's Early Writings," via *Internet*: Full Text Provided by Trustees of the Ellen G. White Publications, Washington D.C: 1963: Host Master: <hitechgroup@rogers.com.> Date of Website Not Found. Homepage: <http://english.sdaglobal.org/>.

University of Michigan and Cornell University, "Making of America" via *Internet*: Homepage: <http://www.hti.umich.edu/cgi/t/text/text...>. Content Added April 2003.

WGBH Boston, producers. "Apocalypse! The Evolution of Apocalyptic Belief and How it Shaped the Western World" PBS: Frontline: November 1999. via *Internet*: <http://www.pbs.org/wgbh/pages/frontline/shows/apocalypse/explanation/doomindustry.html>.

Miscellaneous:

Best, Thomas F. Plenary Lecture. Ecumenical Institute Bossey, Fall Semester, 2004.

Comunita Di Sant'Egidio, Icona dei "Nuovi Martiri," "Attraverso La Grande Tribolazione" Roma: Basilica di San Bartolomeo, all'Isola Tiberina.

Robra, Martin. Interdisciplinary Seminar: Mission and Evangelism/Social Ethics. Ecumenical Institute Bossey, May, 2005.

www.ingramcontent.com/pod-product-compliance
Lightning Source LLC
Chambersburg PA
CBHW070935160426
43193CB00011B/1691